I0606000

TO THE STARS

The Story of NASA

Ron Miller

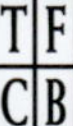

TWENTY-FIRST CENTURY BOOKS / MINNEAPOLIS

This book is dedicated to Sara Ambrose and Hunter Maready.

Twenty-First Century Books™
An imprint of Lerner Publishing Group, Inc.
241 First Avenue North
Minneapolis, MN 55401 USA

For reading levels and more information, look up this title at www.lernerbooks.com.

Main body text set in Columbus MT Std.
Typeface provided by Monotype Typography.

Library of Congress Cataloging-in-Publication Data

Names: Miller, Ron, 1947– author.
Title: To the stars : the story of NASA / Ron Miller.
Description: Minneapolis, MN : Twenty-First Century Books, [2025] | Includes bibliographical references and index. | Audience: Ages 11–18 | Audience: Grades 7–9 | Summary: "From its humble beginnings in the wake of the Space Race to its status as a global leader in space exploration, readers will learn how NASA has been at the forefront of scientific discovery, technological innovation, and international collaboration"— Provided by publisher.
Identifiers: LCCN 2024021602 (print) | LCCN 2024021603 (ebook) | ISBN 9798765648063 (library binding) | ISBN 9798765659403 (epub)
Subjects: LCSH: United States. National Aeronautics and Space Administration—History—Juvenile literature. | Astronautics—United States—History—Juvenile literature. | Aeronautics—United States—History—Juvenile literature. | Outer space—Exploration—United States—History—Juvenile literature.
Classification: LCC TL521 .M458 2025 (print) | LCC TL521 (ebook) | DDC 629.40973—dc23/eng/20240826

LC record available at https://lccn.loc.gov/2024021602
LC ebook record available at https://lccn.loc.gov/2024021603

Manufactured in the United States of America
1-1011025-53368-3/18/2025

Table of Contents

Introduction

Before 1783 no human being had ever left Earth farther than they could jump. That October two brothers, Joseph and Étienne Montgolfier, constructed and launched a huge balloon made of silk and paper and filled with hot air. It carried its lone passenger a few hundred feet above the rooftops of Paris, France. This balloon was tethered to the ground by a rope, but a month later, a similar balloon carried two passengers on a free flight that lasted nearly half an hour and covered 5.5 miles (9 km). For the first time, an artificial device—a machine—allowed humans to fly. Benjamin Franklin witnessed the event and declared that he "could not help feeling a certain mixture of awe and admiration."

Balloons have one major flaw: They cannot be steered. All balloons are lighter than the air around them and are subject to its whims. Like a soap bubble, balloons go where the wind takes them. And without wind, balloons can go nowhere. Attempts to solve this problem resulted in the dirigible, or steerable balloon. These balloons had engines and propellers and could be steered and flown against the wind—if the wind was not blowing too hard.

About 120 years after the Montgolfiers' flight, two other brothers—Orville and Wilbur Wright—invented the airplane, a flying machine that was heavier than the air around it. It was flown and steered under its own power and was not dependent on the wind. The invention of the airplane meant that pilots were no longer limited by the speed and direction of the wind. They could go where they wanted, when they wanted, and at unprecedented speeds.

How a Rocket Works

Physicist Isaac Newton's third law of motion describes how rockets work. It states that for every action there is an equal and opposite reaction. So, if something is pushed forward, something else must move backward by an equal amount. This principle is what allows a rocket to fly. The gases rushing in one direction from the rocket motor create an opposite reaction that propels the rocket in the other direction.

You can try this with a small balloon. After you blow it up, let go of the balloon. The air rushing from it in one direction creates a force propelling the balloon in the opposite direction.

The two basic types of rocket are solid fuel rockets and liquid-fuel rockets, but the principle behind both is the same. In a liquid-fuel rocket, the propellants—the fuel and the oxidizer—are stored separately in liquid form. These are pumped into a combustion chamber where they can burn. In a solid fuel rocket, the propellants are mixed together. The gunpowder used in early rockets is a good example: It's a fuel that contains its own oxidizer. It burns the moment heat is applied.

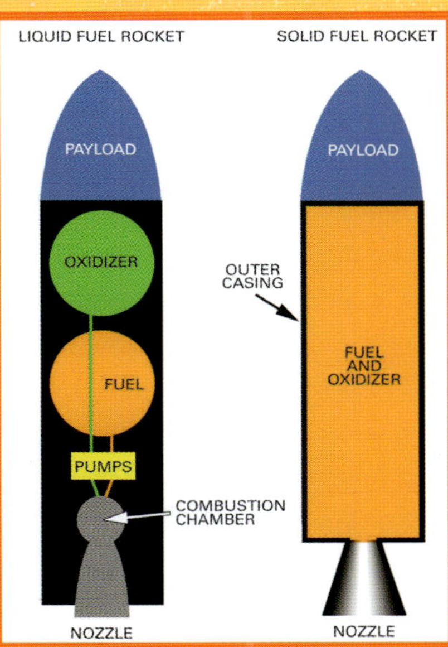

This diagram compares the interior structures of liquid fuel and solid fuel rockets. Each has different advantages and drawbacks, so scientists have to think about which type of rocket to use for missions.

Still, humankind wanted to travel higher and faster. An airplane could travel to almost any point on the surface of the globe, but what about beyond Earth? What about traveling to other planets or the moon? Just as a balloon is dependent on the wind, an airplane depends on an atmosphere to support its wings and provide thrust for its propellers.

In 1865 science fiction writer Jules Verne suggested launching people into space via giant cannons, akin to a rocket. But rocket technology was too primitive at the time to be taken seriously as a method of propulsion for a vehicle. Propelled by gunpowder, rockets were little better than the fireworks seen during Fourth of July celebrations. But in 1926, American engineer Robert Goddard test-flew the first liquid-fueled rocket. The gasoline and liquid oxygen he used provided a much more powerful and reliable source of energy than gunpowder. A liquid-fueled rocket motor could even be turned off and restarted.

With the news of Goddard's invention, scientists, engineers, and dreamers all over the world began to believe that the moon and planets were no longer out of reach. Just eighteen years later, a German V-2 rocket reached an altitude of 109 miles (176 km), well past Earth's atmosphere and into outer space.

Witnessing the developments in flight technology in the early twentieth century, the US government decided to invest in advancing air and space travel. That investment led to the creation of the organization known today as the National Aeronautics and Space Administration (NASA). Since its inception, NASA has contributed invaluable research and technologies to science. From pioneering supersonic flight to landing the first human beings on the moon to creating a giant telescope that unfurled like a flower in space, NASA has spearheaded some of the most incredible scientific projects in history. Let us chart a course through that history and explore the origins, accomplishments, and visions of the organization that dared to reach for the stars.

Chapter 1

NACA

World War I (1914–1918) had broken out across the globe. The sheer scale of this war, involving dozens of nations and resulting in millions of deaths, was unprecedented, and so was the introduction of airplanes to combat.

After the invention of the airplane, the governments of many nations established organizations for aviation research to gain military advantages over their opponents. France, Germany, Russia, and Britain all created special laboratories devoted to developing new materials and techniques. Seeing the progress other nations had made, US President William Howard Taft felt that the country was falling behind.

On December 19, 1912, just nine years and two days after the Wright brothers had flown the first airplane, Taft created the National Aerodynamical Laboratory Commission to make advancements in the science of aviation. But the commission was unable to get support from Congress and was eventually disbanded. The advent of World War I, however, made it all too clear how far behind the United States had fallen. Although they were made of wood and fabric and could carry at most two people, the aircraft flown by German, French, and British pilots were far superior to anything the Americans had. American officials were embarrassed to discover that of the fourteen hundred military aircraft in existence at the beginning of the war, only twenty-three were flown by the United States.

On March 3, 1915, Congress passed Public Law 271, creating the National Advisory Committee for Aeronautics (NACA) "to supervise and direct the scientific study of the problems of flight with a view to their practical solution." NACA was meant to coordinate the various efforts of individual institutions and corporations throughout the United States in developing aviation. The committee would function as a kind of clearinghouse where information could be compiled and shared. It didn't undertake any research of its own, though it did suggest lines of research.

The government's encouragement led to many innovations and developments, such as improved propeller designs and the Liberty engine, one of the most advanced aircraft engine designs in the world at the time. More than twenty thousand Liberty engines were manufactured between 1917 and 1919 and were used in dozens of different aircraft in several nations.

NACA's relatively passive role did not last long. Under the direction of its chair, George W. Lewis, NACA created its own research and testing facility, which began aeronautical research in 1920: the Langley Aeronautical Laboratory, named after Samuel Pierpont Langley (1834–1906), a scientist and inventor whose work was one source of inspiration for the Wright brothers. Lewis, along with John F. Victory (who had been the first employee of the committee), gathered many young scientists and engineers to work at the laboratory, promising them opportunities to pursue even the most fantastic ideas with no strings attached. When the laboratory opened, it employed fifteen technicians and scientists. Five years later, the staff had grown to more than one hundred.

One of the most important research devices the NACA engineers worked on was the wind tunnel. Created by British inventor Francis Wenham in 1871 and developed further by the Wright brothers when they began researching the best designs for their airplane, a wind tunnel is essentially a long tube down which powerful fans force air at high speeds. Engineers can test models of aircraft or wing designs by placing them in the tunnel. Since the air moves past the model instead of the model moving through the air, scientists can study the effectiveness of a shape or design. NACA's wind tunnels enabled its engineers to study the effects of drag, the force that works against an aircraft as it pushes its way through the air. The materials, shape, and size of an aircraft are among the factors that increase or decrease drag. The less drag, the faster and more efficient an aircraft will be because it requires less power to push through the air.

One of the first innovations to reduce drag was the NACA cowling. Many aircraft engines at the time were rotary engines. Instead of the cylinders being in line, like those in the engine of an automobile, the cylinders in a rotary engine surrounded the drive shaft like the spokes of a wheel. This type of engine is very efficient and very powerful . . . but it also presented a problem. The engine was shaped like a big disk and faced the direction in which the plane was traveling. It had to work hard to push itself—and the plane—through the air. In short, it created a lot of drag. NACA engineer Fred Weick developed a cowling, or a kind of hood, that surrounded the engine. It was shaped in such a way that air slid past the engine smoothly, and the cowling added to the aircraft's forward speed.

In 1929 NACA began construction of a very large wind tunnel at Langley. It had a test section 60 feet (18 m) wide and 30 feet (9 m) high, large enough to test an entire full-size aircraft. Going into operation in May 1931, the Full-Scale Wind Tunnel was the largest wind tunnel in the world.

One of the first big successes of this wind tunnel was in 1938 when the US Navy turned to NACA to solve a problem. Its new fighter plane, the XF2A Buffalo, was not performing as well as expected. NACA researchers suspected it was the result of drag and tested it in the wind tunnel. By streamlining the Buffalo—smoothing the surface of the aircraft as much as possible by eliminating bumps, holes, antennas, and other things—engineers were able to increase the top speed of the airplane from 250 to 281 miles (401 to 452 km) per hour.

The success of the tests on the Buffalo led NACA to test nearly eighty aircraft for the army, navy, and air force during World War II (1939–1945), when many new, fast fighter planes were being developed. It opened two more laboratories: the Ames Aeronautical Laboratory in 1939 and the Aircraft Engine Research Laboratory (later renamed for astronaut John Glenn) in 1941. Focusing on propeller design and wing shapes, the labs' work resulted in simpler, more efficient aircraft, such as the P-51 Mustang fighter. As for the Buffalo, it continued contributing to the design of planes, such as the F-22 jet fighter introduced in 2005, until 2010.

The Langley wind tunnel tests a P-51 Mustang fighter plane to help find ways to reduce drag.

Breaking the Sound Barrier

Even before World War II was over, NACA was researching how to take advantage of their new, powerful jet engines and achieve speeds greater than any aircraft had attained before. By 1944 NACA set its sights on designing an aircraft capable of flying faster than the speed of sound.

Engineers had thought such a feat was physically impossible. As an aircraft flies faster, the air in front of the plane compresses and becomes denser, forming something like a wall—or barrier—in front of the plane. Pilots approaching the speed of sound—about 740 miles (1,192 km) per hour at sea level—found their planes acting very strangely. Their planes would start vibrating and become difficult or even impossible to control. Many unexplained crashes were blamed on pilots getting too close to the "sound barrier." Attempting to break through this barrier could be deadly. In England in 1946, a specially designed jet airplane—the de Havilland DH-108, flown by Geoffrey de Havilland, the son of the company's founder—nearly achieved the speed of sound and disintegrated, killing the pilot.

After the war ended, the NACA laboratories made supersonic (faster than the speed of sound) flight their primary goal. Aircraft equipped with the new jet engines that had been developed during the war would be capable of reaching such speeds. But would the aircraft—and their pilots—survive?

Until then, NACA engineers had never designed an aircraft from scratch. Most of their work had been dedicated to improving existing technology, such as making wings, propellers, and engines more efficient. But an aircraft capable of flying faster than sound would have to be an entirely new kind of plane. To create it, NACA collaborated with the US Air Force and the Bell Aircraft Corporation.

The result was a very new sort of aircraft. The Bell X-1 looked like a bullet. It was modeled after machine-gun bullets because they could travel faster than sound and remain intact. The engineers designed the plane to reduce interference with the flow of air around it. The plane was so streamlined that the cockpit was flush with its smooth curves. Even the stubby wings (they spanned only 28 feet [8.5 m] from wingtip to wingtip)

Mach Numbers

Named after Austrian scientist Ernst Mach, a Mach number is the ratio of the speed of an object (such as a jet plane) to the speed of sound in the surrounding medium (such as air). Anything traveling less than Mach 1 is traveling slower than the speed of sound, while anything traveling faster than Mach 1 is traveling faster than the speed of sound. A rocket traveling at Mach 2 is going twice the speed of sound, at Mach 3 three times faster, and so on.

But the speed of sound is not a constant. Sound travels faster in air that is dense or warm than it does in air that is cold or thin. To simplify the influence of these factors, Mach numbers are often calculated assuming the speed of sound at sea level when the air is at a temperature of 59°F (15°C). This makes Mach 1 equal to 761 miles (1,225 km) per hour.

were thin—almost knifelike. And it was small: just 31 feet (9.4 m) long and 10 feet (3 m) tall. Since the X-1 needed to go fast—faster than any propeller-driven aircraft could go—it was rocket-powered. But the rockets used fuel very quickly, so they could only provide thrust for a few seconds, which wasn't long enough for the X-1 to take off under its own power. Instead, it was carried aloft by a much larger plane. A B-29 bomber was specially adapted to carry the rocket plane beneath it, partially inside what had been the bomb bay.

After a series of successful test flights beginning in December 1946 eventually brought the X-1 to Mach 0.8, NACA turned the plane over to the air force. A twenty-four-year-old pilot, Captain Charles (Chuck) Yeager, was chosen to make the first flight past Mach 1. He called the X-1 Glamorous Glennis after his wife and had the name painted on the nose of the plane.

On October 14, 1947, the modified B-29 took off with the X-1 and Yeager aboard. At an altitude of 20,000 feet (6 km), the rocket plane was released. As it dropped away from the bomber, Yeager ignited the rocket engine. As his speed grew closer and closer to Mach 1, he felt the same buffeting and lack of control pilots had been reporting for years whenever they approached the speed of sound. Yeager pressed on. Then, at an altitude of 43,000 feet (13 km), Yeager shot past the sound barrier, reaching a top speed of Mach 1.06—and both aircraft and pilot survived.

The X-Planes . . . Faster and Higher

Emboldened by the success of the X-1, NACA continued developing experimental aircraft over the next decade. Some were rocket-powered like the X-1, while others were propelled by conventional jet engines.

Because the X-1 had required the assistance of another aircraft to reach its top speed, one of NACA's goals was to create an aircraft that not only could exceed the speed of sound but also be able to take off and land under its own power like a conventional airplane. NACA turned to Douglas Aircraft, one of the nation's leading aircraft designers and manufacturers, to come up with a solution.

The result was the Douglas D-558-I Skystreak. About the same size as the X-1—at just 35 feet (10.7 m) long and with a wingspan of 25 feet

(7.6 m)—it was propelled by a powerful turbojet engine that occupied almost all of the available space behind the cockpit. (A turbojet is a jet engine that uses a turbine to compress the air entering the engine before it is mixed with the fuel.) Made largely of aluminum and a magnesium alloy, the Skystreak was strong. It was capable of taking off on its own and withstanding strains eighteen times the force of gravity. Aside from the pilot, the plane carried 500 pounds (230 kg) of instruments that would measure and record every detail of its flight. Unlike the straight-winged X-1 planes, the D-558-I had wings that were sharply swept back, which delayed the beginning of the air compression that formed the sound barrier and allowed the aircraft to reach higher speeds without requiring more powerful engines.

After initial tests, the turbojet engine was replaced by a rocket motor that provided twice the amount of thrust. The new plane was designated the D-558-II Skyrocket. Douglas Aircraft built three D-558-II planes, and the first flight took place on February 4, 1948. By the time the program ended in 1958, the aircraft had made a total of 313 flights. On November 20, 1953, NACA test pilot Albert Scott Crossfield broke through another threshold. Since the turbojet engine that enabled the first Skyrockets to take off under their own power had been replaced by a rocket engine, Crossfield's aircraft had to be carried aloft by a B-29 bomber. After his Skyrocket was released at an altitude of 32,000 feet (9,750 m), Crossfield ignited the rocket engine and the Skystreak shot to 72,000 feet (21,950 m). A few seconds after nosing the plane into a dive, Crossfield became the first human to fly twice the speed of sound, reaching Mach 2.005 (1,526 miles [2,456 km] per hour).

Only a few weeks later, on December 12, Yeager reached a speed of Mach 2.44 flying an X-1A, an improved version of the X-1. These achievements inspired engineers to strive to design even faster aircraft and reach even more impressive speeds. Mach 3 was in sight.

The X-15

With the speed of sound broken, NACA set its sights on ever more incredible achievements. How high could an aircraft fly? Could one break out of Earth's atmosphere? In 1952, NACA began developing a rocket-propelled aircraft capable of reaching the edge of space. Working with the US Air Force and US Navy, NACA created the X-15.

Jet black with short wings set far back along its body, the X-15 looked more like a science fiction spaceship than an aircraft. Since it was designed to operate at the very limits of Earth's atmosphere, it really was more spaceplane than airplane.

The US Air Force and NACA had originally planned to launch the X-15 from the back of one of the air force's Navaho missiles, which would boost the X-15 into Earth orbit. The plane was expected to reach at least four times the speed of sound, which would create tremendous amounts of friction, especially when reentering Earth's atmosphere. Engineers designed a special paint to radiate away the high temperatures created by the friction—hence the aircraft's unusual black color.

At the maximum altitude the X-15 was meant to reach, the atmosphere was forty-five hundred times less dense than at sea level. For all practical purposes, it was a vacuum. That meant dangerous radiation from the sun, normally blocked by Earth's atmosphere, could hurt the X-15's pilots. To protect themselves from such a dangerous environment, the pilots would have to wear space suits not much different from those worn by the astronauts in the later Mercury, Apollo, and Space Shuttle programs. Normal controls for an aircraft wouldn't work in such thin air. Just as a ship's rudder needs water to push against to steer, the rudder and ailerons (movable flaps on the wings) of an aircraft need an atmosphere to work. To give the pilot some control, the X-15 was equipped with eight small rockets in the nose and four in the wingtips. These were fueled by hydrogen peroxide. The pilot could use them to raise or lower the nose of the rocket plane, swing it right or left, or rotate it.

But before the X-15 saw its first flight something happened that changed the world forever.

Chapter 2

The Beep Heard Round the World

In the decade following World War II and with all the incredible advancements in aviation technology, the idea of space travel started appearing in popular media, from books and magazine articles to movies and TV shows. Seemingly everyone began discussing the possibility of humans going to space. If the enthusiastic response to all of this was any indication, the public not only supported future spaceflight but was also confident that it was going to happen soon. After all, NACA's recent experimental flights had reached altitudes previously unattainable.

But the government was not quite so confident. There was no agency devoted specifically to the exploration of space. Instead, these conversations and plans were scattered across various departments, including NACA.

Everything changed on October 4, 1957. Millions of people around the planet turned on their radios to hear a steady *beep, beep, beep* coming from outer space: a signal being transmitted by instruments aboard the world's first artificial satellite. The satellite, they learned, was named Sputnik, the Russian word for "companion." It had been launched by the Soviet Union (a former country that included Russia, Ukraine, and other eastern European nations), and it took the world by surprise.

The announcement of Sputnik was a wake-up call. The United States, which considered itself the world leader in science and technology, had been upstaged by the Soviet Union. The whole world had seen the most powerful, advanced nation beaten by a country that most Americans had believed lagged behind the United States in technological development. Worse yet, the Soviet Union was a Communist country. This was a political and economic system very different from that of the United States and one that many Americans—and most of their leaders—considered a serious threat to the American way of life. To be labeled a Communist was to be labeled "un-American."

It seemed almost impossible that the Communist Soviet Union could beat the democratic, capitalist United States at anything. But if anyone doubted the success of Soviet science and technology, all they had to do was look up at night: They could see a tiny spark of light passing overhead every ninety-six minutes as Sputnik circled Earth.

The Soviet Union launched a second satellite just a month later. Sputnik II carried not only instruments but also a passenger: a dog named Laika. Sputnik I weighed 183 pounds (83 kg), but the new satellite weighed 1,120 pounds (508 kg). With its final booster stage attached, the combined satellite weighed 7,000 pounds (3,175 kg)—almost twice the weight of an average passenger car.

In response to the launch of Sputnik, the United States took a hard look at where it stood in high-altitude research and space exploration. It had to not only catch up but also outrun the Soviet Union to show the world that whatever a nation run by a dictator could do, a free nation such as the United States could do better. To accomplish that, the United States had to focus its ideas, energies, and resources on a single goal: the conquest of space.

With no agency dedicated to space exploration, various branches of the military took up the cause. The navy decided to develop a rocket specially designed for the purpose: the Vanguard. The army decided to adapt an existing ballistic missile called the Redstone, and the air force experimented with a booster rocket called Abel 1.

By December 6, 1957, the navy had its Vanguard rocket ready and scheduled for launch from Cape Canaveral, Florida. The satellite carried in its nose was tiny compared to the Soviet orbiters. It was an aluminum sphere just 6 inches (15 cm) in diameter weighing only 3.2 pounds (1.5 kg).

Nikita Khrushchev, the leader of the Soviet Union, derisively called it an "orange." At 11:44 a.m., the countdown ended and the rocket, its engine roaring, began to lift from the launchpad. Then something went wrong, and the rocket exploded.

The failure was not only a national embarrassment—the United States, which had broadcast its launch on television, had embarrassed itself in front of the entire world. Wernher von Braun, who headed the army's Ballistic Missile Agency—summed it up by saying that after the success of Sputnik and the failure of the first Vanguard, "it became popular to question the bulwarks of our society, our public education system, our industrial strength . . . the capability of our science and technology." He promised to get a satellite into orbit within ninety days of Sputnik's appearance and led the army in adapting the Redstone rocket, one of their ballistic missiles. Unlike the navy's brand-new Vanguard booster, the Redstone rocket had a proven record of reliability. As testament to the Redstone's solid foundation and von Braun's ambition, the new rocket, called the Jupiter-C, successfully boosted a satellite called Explorer 1 into orbit on January 31, 1958. Explorer 1 carried instruments to measure the levels of radiation beyond Earth's atmosphere. They needed to know whether radiation would prove to be a serious hazard to future astronauts.

The navy's accident-plagued Vanguard program eventually caught up, successfully launching a 3-pound (1.4 kg) satellite on March 17, 1958. Vanguard II and III soon followed, the latter putting a 100-pound (45 kg) satellite into orbit.

After such an embarrassing start to the space race, the United States finally regained some morale with these successes. Americans took some solace in that while the Soviet Union had been the first in space, it had placed only two satellites in orbit so far, and the United States was quickly catching up with its increasingly ambitious projects.

NACA Becomes NASA

Later that year, President Dwight Eisenhower announced the National Aeronautics and Space Administration Act. It was America's direct response to the challenge set by Sputnik. "The present National Advisory Committee

Animal Astronauts

Laika the dog who traveled aboard Sputnik II was not the first animal to ride a rocket toward space. That honor belongs to a rhesus monkey named Albert 1, who was launched atop a World War II-era V2 rocket in 1948. The rocket reached an altitude of 39 miles (63 km), but Albert did not survive the flight. A year later, Albert II, also a rhesus monkey, suffered a similar fate. Over the next two or three years, many unfortunate mice and monkeys were launched atop rockets until, finally, on September 20, 1951, eleven mice and a monkey named Yorick were launched nearly 45 miles (72 km) toward space . . . and survived: the first living creatures in history to fly so high and return to Earth safely.

A street dog, Laika became famous for the success of her spaceflight. However, there was no way for her to return to Earth. She died of hyperthermia on her fourth orbit.

Scientists conducted such animal experiments because they were worried about the effects of acceleration during launch and the effects of weightlessness on the human body. Many scientists and doctors doubted that humans could survive prolonged periods of weightlessness. Would the blood circulate properly in the body? Could an astronaut even swallow their food? These and many other questions needed to be answered before a human could be launched into space.

Scientists would figure out the answers by the May 1961 launch of Freedom 7 (see page 26). But first came the extraordinary achievement of a chimpanzee named Ham, who became something of a national celebrity in the United States. Ham became the first chimp in space on January 31, 1961. Launched by the same Redstone booster used by the later Mercury astronauts, Ham reached an altitude of 115 miles (185 km) and a speed of 5,857 miles (9,426 km) per hour. During his 16.5-minute flight, Ham experienced 6.6 minutes of weightlessness. After his return to Earth, Ham retired to, first, the National Zoo in Washington, DC, and then the North Carolina Zoological Park, where he died in 1983. His remains are in the International Space Hall of Fame in Alamogordo, New Mexico.

for Aeronautics (NACA) with its large and competent staff," Eisenhower stated when signing the act on July 29, 1958, "and well-equipped laboratories will provide the nucleus for the NASA. The NACA has an established record of research performance and of cooperation with the armed services. The coordination of space exploration responsibilities with NACA's traditional aeronautical research functions is a natural evolution . . . [one] which should have an even greater impact on our future." NASA would consolidate existing scientific projects and spearhead new developments in space technology. Leading the new agency would be T. Keith Glennan, former head of another scientific government agency, the Atomic Energy Commission.

With the president's signature, NACA no longer existed. It became a brand-new agency known as NASA. It inherited all of NACA's eight thousand employees, its three research laboratories, and its other facilities, as well as the Jet Propulsion Laboratory, which had been under the jurisdiction of the army. Military space projects that were mainly scientific were transferred to the new agency. NASA also took over and consolidated Earth satellite research programs that were until then being conducted separately by the army, air force, and navy. It took two years to reorganize all these projects.

In 1960 NASA presented its first ten-year plan to Congress. This included a timetable to get the first humans in orbit around Earth and the moon, scientific satellites that would collect data about the conditions beyond Earth's atmosphere and the possible dangers of radiation, satellites that would monitor Earth's weather and climate, probes that would provide close-up pictures of Earth's moon and the solar system's other planets, and the development of new launch vehicles. In addition to space exploration, NASA would continue developing innovations in aeronautics.

Hugh Dryden, the first deputy administrator of NASA, listed three goals for the new agency. First, study the environment of space using satellites and space probes. Second, begin the exploration of the solar system by human astronauts. Third, apply space science and technology for the benefit of human welfare.

Eager to show up the Soviet Union, Congress approved these ambitious plans.

NASA Takes Over

On August 17, 1958, just two weeks after the president created NASA, the US Air Force put forth its own project. Abel 1 (later called Pioneer 0) was the first attempt by any nation to launch a spacecraft into deep space as well as the first attempt to reach the moon. But the booster rocket exploded only 73.6 seconds after launch, and the satellite the spacecraft carried was lost.

Two months later, NASA collaborated with the air force on a second attempt: Pioneer 1. The mission was the same as before, to place a satellite in orbit around the moon. But again, a malfunction occurred. The probe reached an altitude of 71,303 miles (114,750 km), but it fell back to Earth only forty-three hours after launch. Although Pioneer 1 failed to reach the moon, it was still able to collect valuable scientific information. Two satellites before it, Explorer 1 and Explorer 3, had detected clouds of radiation surrounding Earth, and Pioneer 1 confirmed the existence of those clouds. The clouds were named the Van Allen belts after James Van Allen, the scientist who discovered their existence after examining the information returned by the Explorer and Pioneer satellites.

Pioneer 1 on the launchpad

NASA had also inherited from NACA the X-15 rocket plane. The X-15 made its first public appearance on October 15, 1958, a year after the launch of Sputnik and only three months after NASA's inception. Two days later, the aircraft was sent to Edwards Air Force Base in Kern County, California, to begin tests. It was ready for an unpowered glide test,

The Jet Propulsion Laboratory

The Jet Propulsion Laboratory had been created in 1936 to research the development of liquid-fueled rockets. It was eventually absorbed by the army, which needed rockets that could assist aircraft in taking off. During World War II and after, it was largely involved in designing missiles for military use. As part of NASA, one of its primary functions is to design and construct the satellites, landers, and rovers that are being used to explore the solar system, its planets and moons, and other objects.

which would test the aircraft's flight characteristics at relatively safe, low speeds. This test took place successfully on June 8, 1959. The first powered flight was made on September 17 that year. The last X-15 flight took place in 1968.

Three X-15 spacecraft were built and flown for a total of 199 flights. The maximum altitude reached by any X-15 was 354,200 feet (108 km) on August 22, 1963. NASA considers outer space as starting at an altitude of 50 miles (80 km), while the Fédération Aéronautique Internationale, which represents the international spaceflight community, puts the line a little bit higher, at 62 miles (100 km). Either way, the X-15 was the first piloted craft to reach space—and its pilots were the world's first astronauts. Eight X-15 pilots were eventually awarded astronaut's wings, the same insignia worn by the men and women who flew Mercury, Apollo, and space shuttle missions. One of the X-15 test pilots was Neil Armstrong, who, as part of the Apollo 11 team, was the first human to set foot on the moon. Another was Joe Engle, who went on to command two space shuttle missions.

Chapter 3

Human Spaceflight

Exactly one year and three days after the launch of Sputnik, NASA announced the ambitious Project Mercury. The goal of the project was to launch not just another satellite into Earth's orbit but also a satellite with a human being aboard. To do this, NASA had to create an entirely new type of spacecraft that could protect its passengers from all of the hazards of outer space—including extreme cold, radiation, and the lack of air—as well as return them safely to Earth after their mission was complete. This was especially challenging because the spacecraft had to be fairly simple and small. NASA intended to use Redstone missiles—the same kind that launched the Explorer missions—to boost the Mercury spacecraft into orbit, so the spacecraft could be no larger or heavier than the rockets could handle.

NASA engineers designed the spacecraft as a kind of shell or capsule that would surround the pilot, who would remain in their seat for the entire duration of their spaceflight. The bell-shaped capsule was about 6 feet (2 m) wide and 10 feet (3 m) tall and weighed about 3,000 pounds (1,361 kg), about as much as an SUV. The interior was barely large enough for both the pilot and all the controls and equipment, which included a total of 7 miles (11 km) of wiring and hundreds of instruments, switches, radios, and lights. Atop the capsule was a tower. At its tip were rocket motors that could carry the capsule out of danger in case of an emergency during takeoff.

Unlike the X-15, which glided to a landing, the wingless Mercury capsule would reenter the atmosphere like a meteor. The gumdrop-like shape was designed to protect the astronaut from the intense heat generated by friction with the atmosphere. The wide, curved base was covered in a thick heat shield that protected the capsule from the heat of reentry through a process called ablation. By flaking off as it burned up, the heat shield material carried the heat away from the spacecraft, and the pilot inside remained safe.

The first flights of the Mercury program were planned to be ballistic, following a curved path like that of a ball thrown into the air. Instead of going into orbit, the capsule would travel up until it reached its maximum altitude of about 100 miles (161 km), then drop back toward Earth.

Segregation in NASA

Although today NASA embraces diversity, claiming that it "is central to the Agency's success through innovation, creativity and contribution of organizations and individuals," this has not always been so. Created in an era when the segregation of races was still commonplace, the first years of NASA saw the agency following the same practices as the rest of the country in the treatment of racial minorities.

But many at NASA understood that people of any race could be scientists. Before the Civil Rights Act became law in 1964, NASA had an office at its Marshall Space Flight Center in Huntsville, Alabama, tasked with employing African Americans in the space industry. A Black NASA specialist toured the country, recruiting Black scientists and engineers, while historically Black colleges were encouraged by the agency to send students to study in the Huntsville area.

Nevertheless, for all of NASA's good intentions, many of its facilities were in the South, where racial prejudice ran deep. The Black engineers, technicians, and scientists might have been welcomed by NASA, but they had a much harder time being accepted by the local communities. That took many years.

Hidden Figures

A century ago, the word *computer* had a very different meaning than it does today. In the 1920s, in the first years after NACA was created, a computer was a human being who solved complex mathematical calculations by hand. Many of these human computers were women, who were thought to be especially adept at doing this kind of work. The first of these women computers were hired by NACA in 1935. With the onset of World War II draining the available workforce, NACA turned to African American women to do these calculations. With segregation still very much a part of American culture, these women were sent to the West Area Computing unit, which was reserved for Black employees. A 1942 memo said, "The engineers admit themselves that the girl computers do the work more rapidly and accurately than they could."

Starting work in 1943, Dorothy Vaughn was one of the early African American women computers to be employed by NACA. By 1949 she was section head of the segregated West Area Computing unit, and when NACA was transformed into NASA, she became an expert at computer language, teaching her male counterparts how to use the new electronic computers.

Katherine Johnson was hired by NACA in 1953 and had to endure the same segregated working conditions as the others. She eventually

Just as NASA was finalizing the manufacturing of its Mercury spacecraft, the Soviet Union took the world by surprise again. On April 12, 1961, a month before the scheduled Mercury launch, Russian pilot Yuri Gagarin became the first human to complete one orbit of Earth.

The so-called space race had become more serious than ever with this public relations setback. NASA felt the increased pressure to get an American into space as soon as possible.

The Mercury 7

The search for astronauts for the Mercury program began in 1958, just after the creation of NASA was announced. Several astronauts would be in the

worked on calculating the flight paths of the Freedom 7 and Friendship 7 missions, often double-checking the calculations made by the electronic computers for accuracy. "You tell me when you want it and where you want it to land," she said, "and I'll do it backwards and tell you where to take off." Johnson's work was a critical part of the success of the Apollo missions to the moon. She retired in 1986, and in 2016 the Katherine G. Johnson Computational Research Facility at Langley Research Center was named in her honor.

Katherine Johnson's calculations reassured astronauts, including John Glenn, that their flight trajectories were safe. At the age of ninety-seven, she was awarded the Presidential Medal of Freedom by Barack Obama in 2015.

program for practical reasons, including that NASA planned several ballistic flights. With so many test flights planned, NASA thought it best to have at least half a dozen astronauts ready. The board tasked with the responsibility of finding potential astronauts decided to look for them in the ranks of military test pilots, whose prior experience in flying and in working with experimental aircraft made them ideal candidates.

One hundred pilots met the requirements for the Mercury program. They were summoned to NASA headquarters in Washington, DC, where they were told about the program. The board asked for volunteers. Fifteen of the hundred chose not to participate. The remainder were put through a grueling battery of tests that included spending hours on a treadmill, having their feet immersed in tubs of ice and having to endure enemas. This narrowed the choice to thirty-two. Out of those, seven men were finally chosen. They were L. Gordon Cooper, Walter Schirra, Alan Shepard, John Glenn, Scott Carpenter, Donald "Deke" Slayton, and Virgil "Gus" Grissom. Reporters deemed them the Mercury 7, a name the crew gladly adopted.

FREEDOM 7

On May 5, 1961, scarcely three weeks after Gagarin's achievement, an American astronaut was launched into space. Astronaut Alan Shepard's Mercury capsule followed a bulletlike ballistic path that lasted only fifteen minutes. Shepard had named his Mercury capsule Freedom 7, the "7" honoring the original seven NASA astronauts. Following his lead, all of the subsequent Mercury astronauts included the number 7 in the names of their spacecraft.

FRIENDSHIP 7

On February 20, 1962, nine months after Shepard's historic flight, Glenn rode into space in Friendship 7. Boosted by an Atlas 6 rocket—a much larger, much more powerful rocket than the Redstone—Glenn achieved Earth orbit, circling the planet three times before returning safely.

While the Mercury program consisted of just six flights into space over two years (two days and six hours in space), it accomplished several major goals. It demonstrated that the human body could withstand the forces of takeoff and reentry and that weightlessness didn't interfere with the astronaut's ability to perform their tasks. Personnel on the ground also gained valuable experience in mission control and communications.

The Mercury 13

While he was testing the astronaut candidates for the Mercury, a former flight surgeon and adviser to NASA named William Randolph Lovelace wondered how women would respond to the same tests. More than two thousand women, most of them teenagers, had already informed NASA that they wanted to join the space program as astronauts. While most of his colleagues scoffed at the idea of female astronauts, Lovelace took the idea seriously. In 1960, 12,400 women had pilot licenses—only 3.6

percent of all pilots in the United States—and many were just as skilled and experienced as the male volunteers.

One of the most promising volunteers was commercial pilot Geraldyn (Jerrie) Cobb. By the time she reached her twenties, Cobb had set new aviation records, including the world altitude record in 1960. Lovelace put Cobb through the same rigorous tests he had the male astronaut candidates undergo. Cobb ranked in the top 2 percent of everyone tested, regardless of their gender. Although these tests were done unofficially, they attracted the interest of NASA, who invited Cobb to become a special consultant. In this new role, Cobb wanted to achieve two goals. One was that NASA continue research "so women's potential contributions to space exploration could be thoroughly investigated and measured," and the other "that the first woman in space be an American, not a Russian."

Later in her life, Jerrie Cobb, pictured here next to a Mercury capsule, spent several decades providing humanitarian aid and charting new aviation routes in the Andes Mountains and Amazon rainforest. She was nominated for a Nobel Peace Prize for her work.

Several members of Congress felt the same way. James G. Fulton, a representative from Pennsylvania, sent a telegram to President Kennedy to "strongly urge immediate U.S. program to put first woman in space as national goal."

After undergoing the same unsanctioned testing as Cobb, thirteen women qualified as potential astronauts. They were immediately dubbed, of course, the Mercury 13.

Qualified they might have been, but the Mercury 13 still faced two huge hurdles. One was the NASA requirement that astronaut candidates have experience flying military jets. At the time, the armed forces didn't allow women to be pilots, and even though several of the thirteen candidates had accumulated more than ten thousand hours flying privately or commercially—three times the amount of time required of male applicants—NASA refused to change the requirement, creating what was essentially a ban on female astronauts. The other hurdle was prejudice. On July 17, 1962, Congress convened a Special Subcommittee on the Selection of Astronauts to discuss admitting women into the national space program. Cobb argued that there were compelling, practical reasons to include women in the astronaut corps. Women weigh less, she pointed out, and consume less oxygen and food. They are more radiation-resistant, less prone to heart attacks, and less susceptible to monotony, heat, cold, pain, and noise than men. Cobb finally pleaded that "we seek, only, a place in our nation's space future without discrimination."

But Mercury astronaut Glenn argued that "men go off and fight the wars and fly the airplanes . . . the fact that women are not in this field is a fact of our social order." Since Glenn was the first American to orbit Earth and a national hero, his opinion put a halt to any possibility of a woman becoming part of any existing NASA space program. Fifteen years later, NASA allowed a woman to become an astronaut.

The Soviet Union, on the other hand, included female astronauts early on. On June 16, 1963, Russian pilot Valentina Tereshkova became the first woman to orbit Earth. NASA finally relented in 1978 with its first class of women astronauts. One of the members was Sally Ride, who in 1983 became the first female NASA astronaut to fly in space. Since then, more than fifty women have flown as NASA astronauts, but while this number may seem large, it accounts for only 14 percent of all Americans who have been sent to space.

Chapter 4

From Earth to the Moon

Only three weeks after Shepard's historic flight into space, President John F. Kennedy announced America's plans to land a man on the moon "before this decade is out." While a journey to the moon had long been a dream of scientists, engineers, and science fiction writers, an international rivalry played an important role. The Soviet Union also had its eyes set on the moon. It was a matter of national pride that the United States not come in second again.

NASA's first step toward a lunar landing had been the Mercury program. It had successfully achieved its main objectives, launching humans into space, learning that they could function effectively while in orbit, and bringing them back alive. By the time the Mercury program ended, only five hundred employees at NASA's Manned Spacecraft Center (later renamed the Johnson Space Center) were still working on it. The remaining two thousand were developing the next two steps toward the moon, the Gemini and Apollo programs.

Gemini

The Gemini program aimed to develop and practice the techniques required for an eventual journey to the moon, which was much more complex than Mercury's task of putting astronauts into Earth orbit. Could astronauts survive being weightless for long periods? Could they rendezvous, or meet up, with another spacecraft and dock with it? Could an astronaut safely leave the spacecraft and "walk" in space? These were some of the questions the Gemini program had to answer before NASA could plan a trip to the moon.

The Gemini spacecraft outwardly resembled the earlier Mercury capsule. But Gemini was a little larger: 1.5 feet (0.5 m) wider at the base and proportionally taller. A Gemini capsule weighed almost three times as much as Mercury, and since it carried two astronauts instead of one, it was still very crowded inside. Unlike the Mercury capsule, the Gemini capsule had emergency ejection seats for its two astronauts instead of an escape tower. The astronauts had to wear parachutes in case of emergency.

Instead of the batteries that powered the Mercury capsule, Gemini contained a pair of fuel cells in an equipment module attached to the base of the capsule. These created electricity through the chemical reaction of hydrogen and oxygen. Since the equipment module would be jettisoned, or detached from the spacecraft, before reentry, the capsule had backup batteries aboard to keep things running as the capsule returned to Earth.

To launch the heavier Gemini spacecraft, the booster was a two-stage Titan 2, a newer, more powerful rocket than either the Redstone or the Atlas used by Mercury.

Rendezvousing with another spacecraft was one of Gemini's most important goals. The technique made reaching the moon practical, because a single rocket capable of traveling to the moon and back would have to be nearly twice the size of the largest rocket built at the time, the Saturn 5. If the United States hoped to beat the Soviet Union to the moon, it needed another solution. NASA engineer John C. Houbolt proposed the idea of breaking the lunar mission into separate segments, each requiring the orbital rendezvous of different spacecraft. To perfect this maneuver, NASA launched an unpiloted spacecraft called Agena into orbit. Then the Gemini astronauts would have to catch up to it and fit the nose of the Gemini capsule into a special docking ring on the Agena.

Such a task required incredible precision. To maneuver this way, the Gemini spacecraft was equipped with several small rocket thrusters. The Mercury astronauts could "steer" their capsules to the degree that they could roll the spacecraft, pitch it up and down, or swing it left and right. By adjusting the direction and strength of the thrusters, the Gemini astronauts had a great deal more control. Since they could move the entire spacecraft up, down, to the sides, backward, and forward, they could fly the capsule almost like an aircraft. When Gemini 6 rendezvoused with Gemini 7 on December 15, 1965, command pilot Wally Schirra was able to fly "rings" around the other spacecraft, safely coming within inches of it.

There was another big difference between the Mercury and Gemini spacecraft. The Mercury capsules simply fell back to Earth like meteors. Once they reentered the atmosphere, the astronaut aboard could not steer the capsule. The Gemini spacecraft, however, reentered at an angle. This created lift, much like that generated by an airplane's wing, giving some measure of control to the astronauts. They could change the point of splashdown, the spot in the ocean where they'd land, by several miles in any direction.

Multistage Rockets

As a rocket travels, its fuel and oxidizer tanks will empty. The empty tanks become dead weight holding the rocket back. If it were possible to cut away the empty part of the fuel tanks as they drain, the rocket would be lighter and could go higher and faster. Engineers came up with a clever way to remove the extra weight: They stacked the rockets in what are called stages.

In a multistage rocket, the first stage is the largest, since it must not only lift itself from the surface of Earth but also all the stages above it. Once it uses up its fuel and oxidizer, it detaches and falls away from the rocket, and the next stage can start its engines. The second stage can be smaller than the first because it only has to lift itself and the stages it carries. Each time an empty stage is jettisoned, the rocket becomes lighter and can go higher and faster.

Stages can be stacked one atop the other, as in the Saturn V, or they can be mounted side by side, as in the space shuttle.

Edward White reportedly had so much fun on his history-making space walk that he didn't want it to end.

In the year and a half that the Gemini program operated, it performed ten crewed missions. Spaceflight became almost routine for mission control, ground crew, and astronauts. After two successful test flights, the first piloted flight, Gemini 3, took place on March 23, 1965. Three months later, on the second piloted Gemini flight, astronaut Edward White made history by being the first American to "walk" in space. Connected to the spacecraft by a tether, White maneuvered using a gas-powered "zip gun" that worked like a handheld rocket motor. The flight also set an endurance record, lasting for four days and completing sixty-two orbits around Earth.

The Gemini program was immensely successful and achieved all its goals but one. NASA originally hoped that the Gemini spacecraft could land on a runway using a special winglike parachute that would allow the astronauts to steer and land the capsule like a glider. Although NASA had developed and tested the parachute system, it couldn't perfect the system within the schedule and had to abandon the plan. The Gemini astronauts made water landings instead, just as the Mercury and later Apollo astronauts did. Despite this, the rendezvous and docking practice was successful, and the Gemini astronauts gained experience at living and working for long periods in the crowded, weightless environment of a capsule flying in space.

Apollo

The Apollo program began with a tragedy.

The very first crewed launch of the Apollo spacecraft, Apollo 1, was set to take place at the end of February 1967. The plan was to test the spacecraft in Earth orbit. On January 27, the Apollo 1 crew, Grissom, White, and Roger Chaffee, were taking part in a preflight test meant to duplicate the conditions leading up to a launch. The astronauts were in space suits, and the capsule was sealed and pressurized. During the test, a flash fire swept through the interior of the Apollo capsule. Although an emergency escape drill was to be part of that day's program, the fire occurred so quickly and the interior of the capsule filled with flames and toxic gases so fast that the astronauts had no time to open the hatches. All three men died.

The tragedy was a terrible setback for NASA. There had already been fifteen test flights of the spacecraft in the Apollo program. Uncrewed tests of the two segments of the spacecraft that would travel to the moon, the Command Module and the Lunar Module, as well as the Saturn launch vehicle had also been successful. NASA had to find out what caused the fire and how to prevent it from happening again. The accident was also a blow to NASA's prestige since it had been justifiably proud of the space program's safety record. Over the following year and a half, NASA implemented new safety measures, such as the installation of a hatch in the Apollo Command Module that could be opened quickly and the removal of flammable materials from inside the module.

Following the Apollo 1 accident, the first crewed flight of Apollo did not occur until October 11, 1968, when Apollo 7 carried astronauts Schirra, Donn Eisele, and Walter Cunningham into Earth orbit. The spacecraft performed perfectly, and the crew performed their experiments successfully. The only serious problem the astronauts had to deal with was a head cold that spread among them shortly after takeoff. The weightless environment made their symptoms worse since their congested sinuses wouldn't drain. Although the men took medication, they were extremely uncomfortable during the entire mission.

Four months later, the crew of Apollo 9 tested the Lunar Module in orbit. Astronauts James McDivitt, David Scott, and Russell Schweickart put the module through all the maneuvers it would have to perform during an actual mission to the moon. Once they confirmed the module was in working order, everything was ready for the first trip to the moon.

At 7:51 a.m. EST on December 21, 1968, Apollo 8, carrying Frank Borman, James Lovell, and William (Bill) Anders, took off from Cape Kennedy. Three days later, on Christmas Eve, the spacecraft went into orbit around the moon.

That evening the astronauts did a live television broadcast from lunar orbit. While they showed viewers back home images of Earth and the moon from space, Lovell told them that "the vast loneliness is awe-inspiring, and it makes you realize just what you have back there on Earth."

The crew took turns reading from the book of Genesis, and they ended the broadcast with Borman signing off with "And from the crew of Apollo 8, we close with good night, good luck, a Merry Christmas, and God bless all of you—all of you on the good Earth."

Living in Space

One of NASA's major concerns in planning crewed missions was keeping its astronauts healthy. Each mission involved the management of oxygen, water, food, and waste.

On the Apollo spacecraft, compressed oxygen was carried in tanks similar to those used by scuba divers or welders. Oxygen comprises only about 20 percent of Earth's atmosphere, but the air inside the Apollo spacecraft was composed of 100 percent oxygen, allowing for lower cabin pressure. But this also presented a fire hazard (as occurred in the Apollo 1 tragedy). Engineers excluded flammable materials inside the capsule and provided emergency masks in case of fire. The carbon dioxide (CO_2) exhaled by the astronauts was filtered from the air by passing it through containers of lithium hydroxide, a chemical that absorbed the CO_2.

Most of the astronauts' food was freeze-dried, with all the water content removed. Some of these foods could be eaten in their freeze-dried form, such as cookies, fruit bars, or cereal. Others needed hot or cold water added. To rehydrate the food, astronauts inserted

For Christmas dinner, the men ate foil-wrapped turkey with cranberry sauce. While Borman thought that most of the food they had been provided was "unappetizing" (being mostly dehydrated), the chunks of turkey were "very good."

The Apollo 8 mission was not only to gain experience in operating the spacecraft and its systems but also to study how a crew performed under the conditions of an actual trip to the moon. While in orbit around the moon, the crew photographed the surface—including the side invisible from Earth—gathering information about the condition of the lunar landscape for future landings.

Apollo 10 was another practice run to the moon and back. Launched May 18, 1969, Thomas Stafford, John Young, and Eugene Cernan made the round trip, returning to Earth on May 26, 1969. While orbiting the moon, Young remained in the Command Module as Stafford and Cernan took the Lunar Module to about 9 miles (14 km) above the surface of the moon.

the nozzle of the water supply into a special opening in the plastic bag containing the food. After mixing the food with the water, the astronauts could squeeze it into their mouths through a tube.

Like on Gemini, the Command Module's fuel cells created electricity by combining oxygen and hydrogen. A by-product of this process was water, which the astronauts could drink.

Urine was collected by a special undergarment that transferred the fluid to a tank. Fecal matter was collected in a plastic bag that was in turn sealed inside a second bag. The Command Module contained a sanitation box to store these bags.

Exercise was important too. In a weightless environment, bones tend to lose mass since they don't need to support the body. Exercise is important to retain bone strength. Because space was so limited inside the Apollo Command Module, exercising had to be limited to stretching using a small device that allowed the astronauts to pit one muscle against another.

They tested the performance of the module's descent and ascent engines, the landing and rendezvous radars, and the communication systems. They passed closely over the site in the Sea of Tranquility that was planned for the Apollo 11 landing, taking detailed photographs to make sure the site was safe. The ideal location would be relatively smooth and level with few, if any, rocks and small craters, reducing the risk of the module tipping over or breaking.

On the Moon

Apollo 11 took off at 8:32 a.m. on July 16, 1969. Aboard were astronauts Armstrong, Michael Collins, and Edwin "Buzz" Aldrin. Three days later, they were orbiting the moon. On July 20, Armstrong and Aldrin entered the Lunar Module they had dubbed the Eagle and began the descent to the lunar surface. It took less than thirteen minutes to reach it. When the lander was less than 1,700 feet (500 m) above the surface, Armstrong noticed that the onboard computer was steering the spacecraft to a landing in an area that looked much too rough to be safe. Large boulders were scattered everywhere. The module could tip over or get damaged on such an uneven surface. Taking over the controls, Armstrong steered the Lunar Module to a safer-looking spot.

At 3:17 p.m., Armstrong called mission control back in Houston, Texas. "Tranquility Base here," he announced. "The Eagle has landed."

At 9:56 p.m., Armstrong climbed down the ladder attached to one of the landing legs and set foot on the lunar surface. "That's one small step for a man," he radioed to Houston, "one giant leap for mankind."

Followed a few minutes later by Aldrin, the astronauts spent two and a half hours exploring the surface of the moon, never straying more than 20 feet (6 m) from the lander. They gathered samples of rocks and soil as well as data from several scientific instruments. They also erected a United States flag and unveiled a commemorative plaque that had been attached to one of the legs of the lander. The inscription on the plaque read, "Here men from the planet Earth first set foot upon the moon, July 1969 A.D. We came in peace for all mankind." They left it on the surface along with the flag.

In addition to walking on the surface of the moon, the Apollo 11 astronauts conducted scientific experiments. Here, Buzz Aldrin is taking measurements of the solar wind.

After spending just over twenty-one hours on the moon, Aldrin and Armstrong returned to the orbiting Command Module. After rendezvousing with the Command Module, the astronauts transferred to it from the Lunar Module. The two spacecraft then separated, with the Command Module headed back to Earth while the Lunar Module remained in orbit around the moon and likely later crashed into it. The three astronauts splashed down in the Pacific Ocean not far from Hawai'i on July 24, after a journey of eight days and three hours to the moon and back.

The Other Apollos

There were five more missions to land on the moon after Apollo 11. NASA had planned on six, but Apollo 13 suffered a malfunction when an oxygen tank in the Service Module exploded. The spacecraft was 200,000 miles (321,800 km) from Earth, well on its way to the moon. With the spacecraft damaged so severely, the mission changed from landing on the moon to getting the crew back home alive.

The explosion had destroyed both of the tanks that supplied oxygen to the Command Module. The crew, Lovell, Fred Haise, and Jack Swigert, were forced to retreat into the Lunar Module, where they could survive on its supplies. The module, however, was designed to support two people for two days, not three for nearly four days. The men had to ration their daily water intake to just 6 ounces (170 g) each. Power was rationed too, and the temperature inside the cabin of the Lunar Module fell to below 40°F (4°C). As the crew breathed, they exhaled CO_2, and dangerous quantities were starting to accumulate in the cramped space. The Command Module had canisters of lithium hydroxide, a chemical that absorbed CO_2, but they would not fit into the Lunar Module. After a lot of head-scratching, mission control devised a way to use plastic bags, cardboard, and duct tape to adapt the containers.

As the astronauts approached Earth for reentry, mission controllers looked to the skies with worry. The explosion could have damaged the Command Module's heat shield. If this were true, the capsule would burn up on entry, killing the astronauts. There was nothing to do but watch and wait.

The Apollo 13 astronauts were rescued by the USS *Iwo Jima*. President Richard Nixon awarded the mission's operation crew the Presidential Medal of Freedom for their efforts in returning the astronauts home safely.

The Apollo landing sites are charted on this image of the moon, along with how long the Lunar Modules (LM) stayed on the surface and how long astronauts conducted extravehicular activities (EVA).

The reentry occurred without incident, and the three astronauts returned safely to Earth.

The other Apollo missions were without incident. Apollo 12 (November 14 to 24, 1969) landed not far from the Surveyor 3 robotic lander that NASA had sent two and a half years earlier. The astronauts collected pieces of Surveyor to see what changes might have occurred to materials exposed to conditions on the moon for two and a half years. They also set up experiments to detect moonquakes, the moon's equivalent of earthquakes, and the moon's magnetic field.

Like Apollo 11 and 12, the crew of Apollo 14 (January 31 to February 9, 1971) collected samples of lunar soil and rocks—more than 90 pounds (40 kg) of the stuff. One of the two astronauts who landed on the moon during this mission was Shepard, the first American to fly into space. The crew spent thirty-three and a half hours on the moon, of which nine hours and twenty-three minutes were spent exploring the surface. They also left instruments that radioed information about conditions on the moon back to Earth. These included a seismometer that went on to detect thousands of moonquakes, giving scientists clues about the internal structure of the moon.

Why Did NASA Stop Apollo?

The Apollo lunar landing program was very expensive. The first mission, Apollo 11, cost $335 million. The entire program cost $25.8 billion. This was one of the reasons for stopping the program after Apollo 17. Another, and perhaps more important, reason was that the American public was losing interest. After the thrill of the first moon landing and the suspense of Apollo 13, travel to the moon seemed to become almost as safe and routine as a tourist flying from across the country. Americans simply weren't as excited for the seventh lunar landing as the first one.

The rivalry between the United States and the Soviet Union that had driven the space race had also cooled down. The Soviets had abandoned their plans to land on the moon, so the United States no longer had anything to prove. With the US government's attention turned toward the Civil Rights Movement and the nationwide protests erupting against the Vietnam War (1954–1975), one more mission to the moon didn't seem as important in comparison.

Apollo 15 (July 26 to August 7, 1971) set down near Hadley Rille, a ravine 1,300 feet (400 m) deep and nearly a mile (1.5 km) wide. Nearby were the 3-mile-high (5 km) Montes Apenninus. Astronauts James Irwin and Scott spent sixty-seven hours on the moon, going for moonwalks three times. And they had the advantage of a Lunar Roving Vehicle. Powered by batteries, the rover could travel up to 8 miles (13 km) per hour, greatly extending the area the astronauts could explore.

While Apollo 16 (April 16 to 27, 1972) Mission Commander Thomas Mattingly remained in orbit, Young and Charles Duke spent seventy-one hours on the moon, twenty of them exploring on foot or on the Lunar Roving Vehicle. They set out several experiments on the surface, including seismometers, an experiment to measure heat flowing from the core of the moon, a cosmic ray detector that measured energetic particles emitted by distant stars and galaxies, and a device to measure the content of the solar wind, a flow of charged particles called plasma coming from the sun. They also took photos of selected stars, measured the moon's magnetic field, and gathered 211 pounds (95.7 kg) of samples to take back to Earth. One of the rocks, weighing 25 pounds (11.3 kg), was the largest ever brought back from the moon. The astronauts covered 16.7 miles (26.9 km) in the rover, traveling nearly 3 miles (4.6 km) from the lander.

Apollo 17 (December 7 to 19, 1972) landed in the Taurus-Littrow region of highlands and valleys. While the Command Module pilot, Ronald Evans, remained in orbit, Cernan and Harrison Schmitt made a precision landing fewer than 800 feet (240 m) from the planned target. Schmitt had a doctorate in geology and was the first scientist to set foot on the moon. He and Cernan spent more time on the moon than any other Apollo astronauts before them. As their predecessors did, they set up experiments on the surface and gathered samples, 242 pounds (110 kg) in all.

Schmitt and Cernan were the last humans to set foot on the moon. With their safe return, the Apollo program was over. More than forty years later, NASA began to think seriously about returning to the moon.

Chapter 5

The Space Shuttle

Long before the end of the Apollo program, NASA had begun looking for a reusable launch system. All the boosters that had launched Mercury, Gemini, and Apollo into orbit had been disposable. They were used once and allowed to fall back to Earth. This was very wasteful. NASA couldn't afford to keep throwing away $110 million rockets. It needed to design and build a spacecraft that could shuttle personnel and supplies to and from space. Thus began the Space Shuttle program.

NASA engineers had two problems to solve: how to get a shuttle into orbit and how to get it back safely. A capsule like Gemini or Apollo, which reentered the atmosphere ballistically and descended by parachute, wouldn't work. The planned shuttle would be much too large for a parachute landing. They realized it would have to be some sort of winged spacecraft, like the X-15, that could reenter the atmosphere and glide to landing, setting down on a runway like an ordinary airplane. Wings, though, presented a potential problem. Since they are the thinnest part of an aircraft, they are the most vulnerable to the tremendous forces and intense heat encountered during reentry.

Lifting Bodies

To avoid the challenge of engineering wings that could withstand the physical stresses of reentry, researchers sought to create a spacecraft that could be flown and landed like an aircraft but did not have any wings. The result was a strange-looking aircraft called a lifting body. Instead of wings providing the lift that enables an airplane to fly, the body of the aircraft itself had a very special shape, one that enabled it to create enough lift to fly and be maneuvered like an ordinary airplane.

Alfred J. Eggers Jr. of NACA's Ames Aeronautical Laboratory (now NASA's Ames Research Center) suggested the idea for lifting bodies in 1957. NACA had been researching how the nose cones of missiles acted when returning to Earth from high altitudes. Eggers found that by modifying the shape of the cone to be flatter on one side, it would produce lift, much like a wing, instead of simply plunging through the atmosphere like a meteor.

Wind tunnel tests of the shape, which Eggers designated the M-1, showed that it worked very well, even at speeds of up to 17,500 miles (28,175 km) per hour. But it did not produce enough lift at slower speeds, such as those required for safely landing. And the M-1's sharp, pointed nose created friction with the air and produced heat that could damage the craft or even destroy it.

Another NACA researcher, H. Julian Allen, had discovered that a rounded, blunt-nosed shape worked better than one with a sharp point. The blunt nose pushed air aside, reducing the friction on the rest of the spacecraft, while a sharp nose let air slide along the spacecraft, increasing friction. Allen's research helped engineers design the Mercury capsule, which reentered the atmosphere blunt end first. So NACA incorporated the shape into its work on lifting bodies.

The result of Eggers's and Allen's work was the M-2, one of the strangest-looking aircraft ever developed. It was shaped like a cone split in half, with a blunt nose and two tail fins that gave the pilot control over steering the spacecraft. Its pilots quickly dubbed it "the flying bathtub."

NASA inherited the lifting body project from NACA. In 1963 NASA constructed a full-size test model, called the M2-F1. (The "M" was for "manned" and the "F" for "flight version.") Unsure whether it would be safe to fly, NASA first tested the aircraft as an unpiloted, unpowered glider. A specially adapted B-52 bomber carried the prototype high into the sky and then released it. It glided safely down to the ground. The results were very successful—the M2-F1 made 477 test flights—and engineers constructed an improved version based on what they had learned. Some of these improvements included relocating the cockpit and installing retractable landing gear. The new craft, the M2-F2, appeared in 1965. By 1967 it had made sixteen subsonic flights—flights at speeds below Mach 1. All of these flights, of both the M2-F1 and M2-F2, were unpowered. But simply gliding away from the B-52 bomber, the M2-F2 reached speeds of up to Mach 0.7.

After an accident badly damaged the M2-F2, it was rebuilt with numerous improvements—most notably a third vertical stabilizer—and given a new name: M2-F3. NASA equipped the M2-F3 with reaction jets, similar to those used in the X-15 for when ordinary controls failed to function at the limits of Earth's atmosphere, in addition to its conventional aircraft controls. The M2-F3 completed its first powered flight on November 25, 1970. The aircraft flew twenty-six times between 1970 and

The M2-F2's final flight ended with a crash landing. Its pilot, Bruce Peterson, had to maneuver the aircraft to avoid colliding with a helicopter and lost control of the landing. He recovered from the crash but lost vision in his right eye.

1972, reaching a top altitude of 71,500 feet (22 km) and a top speed of Mach 1.6 (1,064 miles, or 1,712 km, per hour).

Encouraged by the M2-F3's success, NASA ordered the design and construction of an even further improved lifting body, the HL-10 ("HL" stands for "Horizontal Landing"). It was equipped with a rocket engine, but to ensure the spacecraft could withstand falling through the atmosphere, NASA first tested it as a glider. The HL-10 made thirty-seven flights, and with the assistance of its powerful engine, it achieved speeds of Mach 1.86 (1,228 miles, or 1,976 km, per hour) and altitudes of up to 90,030 feet (27 km).

In the late 1960s, NASA collaborated with the air force on two lifting body programs, the X-24A and X-24B, to further evaluate the reliability of wingless aircraft and to test the use of a lifting body as a reentry vehicle in spaceflight. NASA used this information to design the space shuttle. Although the space shuttle appears to have wings, it is really a lifting body. It depends not only on its wings to provide lift when gliding back into the atmosphere but also the shape of its entire fuselage (the main body of an aircraft).

Reentry: Getting Back to Earth

When the spacecraft in the Mercury, Gemini, and Apollo programs reentered Earth's atmosphere, they were traveling very fast. The Apollo Command Module reentered at 25,000 miles (40,225 km) per hour, heating to 5,000°F (2,760°C) due to friction with the atmosphere. Temperatures that high would cause a spacecraft to quickly burn up if it weren't protected by a heat shield.

NASA had already experimented with the problem of reentry with the X-15. When reentering the atmosphere after its flights into space, friction from the air heated the spaceplane's exterior to 1,202°F (650°C). The spaceplane was protected from these high temperatures by being made of a special metal, an alloy of chrome and nickel called Inconel X-750. A shuttle returning from orbit would be traveling at even greater speeds: 17,500 miles (28,158 km) per hour, or Mach 25. This would create temperatures of up to 3,000°F (1,649°C).

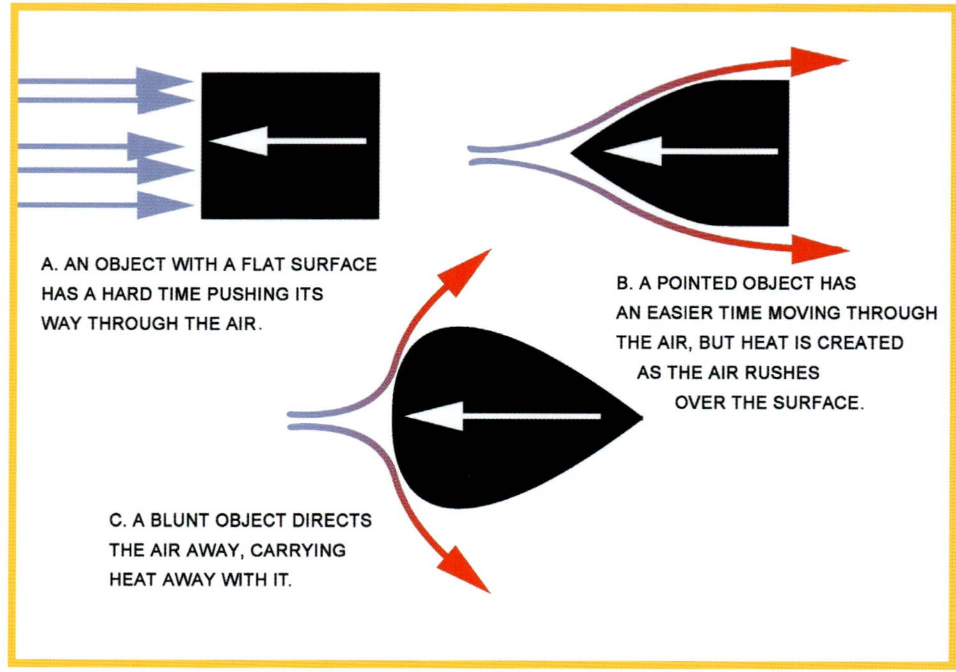

This diagram shows how air moves around different shapes. While a pointed shape helps an aircraft move through the air quickly, a blunter shape is safer because it carries the heat generated by friction away from the aircraft.

Since the shuttle was so much bigger than the early space capsules and traveling so much faster, the heat shield and alloy would not be enough to protect it from burning up on reentry. Instead, the entire underside of the space shuttle—the side that would be facing the atmosphere as the spacecraft returned to Earth—was covered with special tiles made of silicone. The leading edges of the wings were covered by a composite material made of carbon-carbon. This special form of carbon is not only very strong but also highly resistant to heat.

Wings into Space

NASA eventually settled on a design where a large, winged spacecraft—a spaceplane—would take off using its own engines with the aid of a pair of disposable booster rockets. The main fuel tank for the spaceplane would be separate from the plane and would be discarded once it was empty.

Space shuttle launches were exciting events that many people watched in person at Cape Canaveral—from a safe distance, of course.

When its mission was completed, the spaceplane—without fuel—would return to Earth as a glider. It could then be reused over and over. They called it the Space Transportation System, colloquially known as the space shuttle.

The space shuttle was the largest spacecraft yet to be flown into space: 120 feet (37 m) long with a wingspan of 80 feet (24 m). It was a lot like a big truck. The main body of the space shuttle—virtually all of the space between the cockpit, located in the nose, and the engines at the rear—was a cargo bay 60 feet (18 m) long and 15 feet (4.6 m) wide, nearly big enough to hold two school buses. The shuttle could carry up to 65,000 pounds (29,480 kg)—over 32 tons, 29 t—of cargo into orbits between 230 miles and 690 miles (370 km to 1,110 km) above Earth. The cargo might be a single payload—such as a large satellite—or many smaller items. The astronauts could also retrieve a broken or damaged satellite from orbit and return it to Earth for repair.

The crew included three astronauts and up to four mission specialists, who were often scientists or the engineers and technicians needed to manage a payload.

Between the first shuttle launch, on April 12, 1981, and the landing of the final shuttle on July 21, 2011, the program flew 135 missions. All of them accomplished something significant, from launching satellites and the Hubble Space Telescope to performing science experiments and helping build the International Space Station. Some of the most memorable missions include the following:

Space shuttles opened their cargo bays to dock with the International Space Station and deliver their payloads.

- April 12, 1981—STS-1, Columbia, was the first space shuttle NASA launched into orbit. It was also the first spacecraft to return to Earth as a glider, landing on a runway like a conventional aircraft.
- June 18, 1983—STS-7, Challenger, carried the first American woman, astronaut Sally Ride, into space, twenty years after Russian Valentina Tereshkova's historic flight. During the flight, Ride helped her fellow astronauts deploy two communications satellites from the shuttle's cargo bay.
- August 30, 1983—STS-8, Challenger, carried the first African American astronaut, Guion Bluford. He helped place a communications satellite and a weather satellite into orbit.
- February 3, 1984—STS-41B, Challenger, flew astronauts Bruce McCandless II and Robert L. Stewart to space to test the Manned Maneuvering Unit. This was a kind of rocket-powered backpack that allowed the astronauts to move around in space unattached to

their spacecraft. When Gemini astronaut White became the first American to walk in space (preceded by Russian cosmonaut Alexei Leonov), he was tethered to his spacecraft so there would be no danger of floating off into space. Because they weren't tethered to Challenger while wearing the Manned Maneuvering Unit, McCandless and Stewart became, in effect, spacecraft themselves: the first human satellites of Earth.

- April 29, 1990—STS-31, Discovery, launched the Hubble Space Telescope. The telescope sent back extraordinarily detailed pictures of stars and galaxies, but they weren't as good as they could be. There was a problem with one of the mirrors in the instrument. The telescope was designed to be serviced while in orbit so a later shuttle mission was able to repair it. The Hubble Space Telescope was serviced five different times by space shuttle crews. Still in operation more than thirty years later, the space telescope has helped astronomers to understand the evolution and formation of galaxies, found supermassive black holes in the centers of most galaxies, and mapped the presence of the mysterious dark matter that makes up most of the universe we live in, among many other accomplishments.
- June 29, 1995—STS-71, Atlantis, was the first American spacecraft to dock with the Russian space station, Mir. The shuttle carried two Russian astronauts to the station and picked up an American astronaut and two cosmonauts for their return to Earth.
- October 29, 1998—STS-95, Discovery, carried the oldest astronaut into space: Glenn, aged seventy-seven. He was making his second flight into space after being the first American to orbit Earth in 1962.
- December 4, 1998, to June 1, 2011—The International Space Station is constructed. Taking advantage of the shuttle's huge cargo bay, most of the large components of the space station were carried into space by thirty-six individual space shuttle missions.
- July 21, 2011—STS-135, Atlantis, returned to Earth, completing the final space shuttle mission. It was the thirty-third flight for the Atlantis.

Disasters

The word *disaster* comes from Latin and means "ill-starred." It seems especially appropriate when talking about the tragedies that occurred in the history of spaceflight.

NASA had endured many terrible accidents in the past, but the loss of the crew of Apollo 1 was the first fatality. Many years went by before another deadly tragedy occurred.

The year 1986 was going to be a busy one for the space shuttle. Fifteen missions were planned, including the launch of the Hubble Space Telescope. The first mission, STS-61C, launched on January 12. The next launch, STS-51L, was to be the twenty-fifth mission in the Space Shuttle program and the tenth flight for the Challenger. The plan was for the space shuttle to remain in orbit for six days. The crew consisted of Michael J. Smith, Francis R. (Dick) Scobee, Ronald E. McNair, Ellison S. Onizuka, Gregory B. Jarvis, and Judith A. Resnik. A special member of the crew was Christa McAuliffe, who unlike the others was not a pilot or scientist. Two years earlier, President Ronald Reagan had announced the Teacher in Space Project, which would send an ordinary educator into orbit on a space shuttle. Ten thousand teachers from all over the United States applied. From that list, NASA selected ten applicants to undergo medical tests at Johnson Space Center in Houston. On July 19, 1985, Vice President George H. W. Bush announced the winner of the competition: McAuliffe, a middle school teacher from New Hampshire.

During the six-day mission, McAuliffe would conduct lessons for schoolchildren from orbit while the rest of the crew deployed a communications satellite and satellites that would study Halley's Comet.

After a few delays in the launch schedule, the astronauts boarded Challenger on January 28, 1989. NASA personnel were worried about the unusually cold temperatures that had occurred overnight, temperatures cold enough to form ice on the launch tower. Even more of a worry was the effect of the cold on the gaskets—called O-rings—that sealed the separate segments of the solid fuel boosters. If one of these gaskets were to fail, flame from the burning rocket fuel could escape from the sides of the booster. Despite these concerns, the Challenger was cleared for takeoff at 11:38 a.m. (EST).

Star Trek, NASA, and the Space Shuttle

NASA planned to name the first space shuttle orbiter Constitution because it would be presented to the public on September 17, 1976, the anniversary of the ratification of the United States Constitution. But fans of the television series *Star Trek* had other ideas. They bombarded NASA with letters pleading with the agency to name the orbiter Enterprise, after the starship in the show. Struck by the fans' enthusiasm, President Gerald R. Ford directed NASA to give the first space shuttle a new name, Enterprise. The original cast members of the series, as well as *Star Trek*'s creator, Gene Roddenberry, were invited to the ceremony where the newly christened Enterprise rolled out of the plant in which it had been built. Throughout 1977, the Enterprise conducted test flights in Earth's atmosphere to ensure future space shuttles could take off and land safely. Enterprise never saw spaceflight, but the tests it completed helped NASA design the final space shuttles.

NASA later commissioned actor Nichelle Nichols, who portrayed Lieutenant Nyota Uhuru on *Star Trek*, to create a video encouraging women and minorities to apply to become space shuttle astronauts. The campaign worked: In 1978, when NASA announced the names of thirty-five new astronauts, women and minorities were represented for the first time.

The launch appeared to proceed normally, but just seventy-three seconds after liftoff the Challenger disappeared in a ball of fire. The space shuttle had exploded, and all seven astronauts died.

One of the O-rings had failed. A jet of flame shooting from the opening had ignited the big external fuel tank, which then exploded like a bomb.

After the tragedy, NASA canceled the Teacher in Space Project. It would be many years before NASA regained the confidence to send ordinary citizens into space. As a replacement for the Teacher in Space Project, it created the Educator Astronaut Project in 2004. Qualified teachers would be trained as full-time astronauts rather than payload specialists, a much more minimal role. Joseph M. Acaba, Richard R. Arnold, and Dorothy Metcalf-Lindenburger became the first three educator astronauts. All three have successfully completed space shuttle missions. Acaba and Arnold have also been aboard the International Space Station. In 2020 NASA named Acaba as a member of the team of astronauts who will travel to the moon in the Acceleration, Reconnection, Turbulence and Electrodynamics of the Moon's Interaction with the Sun (ARTEMIS, called Artemis) lunar landing program.

The loss of Challenger and its crew was not the last tragedy in the history of the space shuttle. In 2003 Columbia, NASA's oldest orbiter, was returning to Earth after performing a sixteen-day mission in space. The seven-member crew had completed eighty experiments in the Research Double Module, a self-contained laboratory carried in the space shuttle's cargo bay. As the astronauts were reentering the atmosphere on February 1, the Columbia disintegrated. Astronauts David M. Brown, Rick D. Husband, Laurel B. Clark, Kalpana Chawla, Michael P. Anderson, William C. McCool, and Ilan Ramon died.

Investigation of the wreckage of the space shuttle and footage of the accident revealed that a piece of the foam insulation that protected the big external fuel tank had broken loose during takeoff. This had struck the space shuttle's left wing, damaging it. The extreme heat and forces encountered during reentry caused further damage, which compounded quickly, and the entire space shuttle broke apart like a meteor.

A year after the Columbia disaster, President George W. Bush declared that NASA "will return the space shuttle to flight as soon as possible, consistent with safety concerns and the recommendations of the Columbia Accident Investigation Board. The Shuttle's chief purpose over the next several years will be to help finish assembly of the International Space Station." He then announced the end of the Space Shuttle program, saying that "in 2010, the space shuttle—after nearly 30 years of duty—will be retired from service." The Space Shuttle program officially closed July 21, 2011, when the space shuttle Atlantis made its final landing.

Chapter 6

Space Stations

A space station is a satellite large enough for people to live and work in for extended periods. Unlike the Gemini or Apollo capsules that carried a crew into orbit and then returned with the same crew a few days later, space stations remain in orbit for much longer. Different crews inhabit them, coming and going as needed using other spacecraft, such as the space shuttles. Orbiting Earth for months or even years, scientists aboard a space station can study Earth as well as the environment of space just beyond Earth's atmosphere. The idea for such a satellite goes back to the 1920s, and creating a station in space was always one of NASA's goals.

The Soviet Union launched the first space station, Salyut 1, on April 19, 1971. The station remained in orbit for less than a year, and for most of that time, it was unused. When it ran out of fuel in October 1971, the Soviets directed it back into Earth's atmosphere to burn up. Meanwhile, NASA, looking for an inexpensive sequel to Apollo, decided to use leftover Apollo hardware to create a permanently orbiting station.

Skylab

Although the giant Saturn 5 rocket had been designed for the Apollo lunar landing program, engineers realized that they could put it to a different use.

After removing the Command Module and lunar lander, they launched the third stage by itself into Earth orbit to function as a space station. Named Skylab, the main body of the space station was a cylinder nearly 56 feet (18 m) long and 22 feet (6.7 m) wide, the size of a small house. It was very much like one in space, divided into two levels with bedrooms, a kitchen, a bathroom (with a toilet and shower), and work areas. Solar panels attached to the sides of the station like huge wings provided plenty of electricity. At one end of the station was an adapter that allowed Apollo Command Modules to dock and their astronauts to leave the capsules and enter the station. Attached to one side of the adapter was the Apollo Telescope Mount, an observatory designed to study the sun, which had its own array of solar panels.

The whole thing weighed over 100 tons (91 t). It was called Skylab.

Skylab was launched into an orbit 270 miles (434 km) above Earth on

The First Ideas for a Space Station

The first person to write about an inhabited Earth satellite was author Edward Everett Hale in 1869. In his short novel *The Brick Moon*, Hale described the launch of a huge, spherical satellite carrying a crew of forty men and women. Hale anticipated many of the potential uses such a station might have. As a permanently visible object in the night sky, it served as a navigational aid for ships. The crew observed Earth from space and transmitted information about weather and geography to scientists on the ground.

In 1929 engineer Herman Potočnik proposed a space station that seems very modern today. His station would orbit 22,370 miles (36,000 km) above Earth, as a large donut-shaped wheel about 100 feet (30 m) across. Rotating the wheel would provide artificial gravity for the crew. To support the crew's well-being and scientific activities, the station would include cabins, a dining room, laboratories, a photographic darkroom, lavatories, and a laundry area. It would have hot and cold running water. Potočnik envisioned a space telescope orbiting separately nearby. From

May 14, 1973. Over the next nine months, three different crews, each with three astronauts, inhabited the station. They studied the sun and observed Earth and a passing comet. NASA also held a national competition for high school students to submit experiments for the astronauts on Skylab to perform. Out of the thirty-five hundred experiments submitted, NASA selected twenty-five. These experiments included the study of the effects of low gravity—or microgravity—on the behavior of living cells, the shape of spiderwebs, the action of fluids, and the growth of bacteria. The astronauts also studied the effects on the human body of living in space for extended periods, valuable information for future long-term spaceflights, such as a trip to Mars.

The final crew left Skylab in 1974. The empty station's orbit slowly decayed, slowing down and getting closer and closer to Earth, until it finally reentered Earth's atmosphere and burned up on July 11, 1979.

the telescope, crews could observe Earth, other planets in the solar system, and the moon. Power for the station and observatory would come from a solar generator, a machine that transforms energy from the sun into electricity.

Potočnik even suggested that his station would be maintained by a fleet of winged shuttles that would be launched from Earth by large boosters, very much like NASA's later space shuttles.

In the 1950s, former Nazi scientist, then working for NASA, Wernher von Braun designed a space station that resembled Potočnik's. Von Braun's was an enormous wheel 250 feet (76 m) in diameter, housing a crew of several hundred astronauts, and it too would be maintained by a fleet of shuttles. He selected the Air Proving Ground Command in Florida as the potential launch site for the shuttles. This was a prescient choice: The site eventually became the Kennedy Space Center, NASA's primary launch site. Von Braun's station would not only observe Earth but also would be an orbiting base for expeditions to the moon and Mars. Von Braun expected a space station like this to be in orbit by 1963.

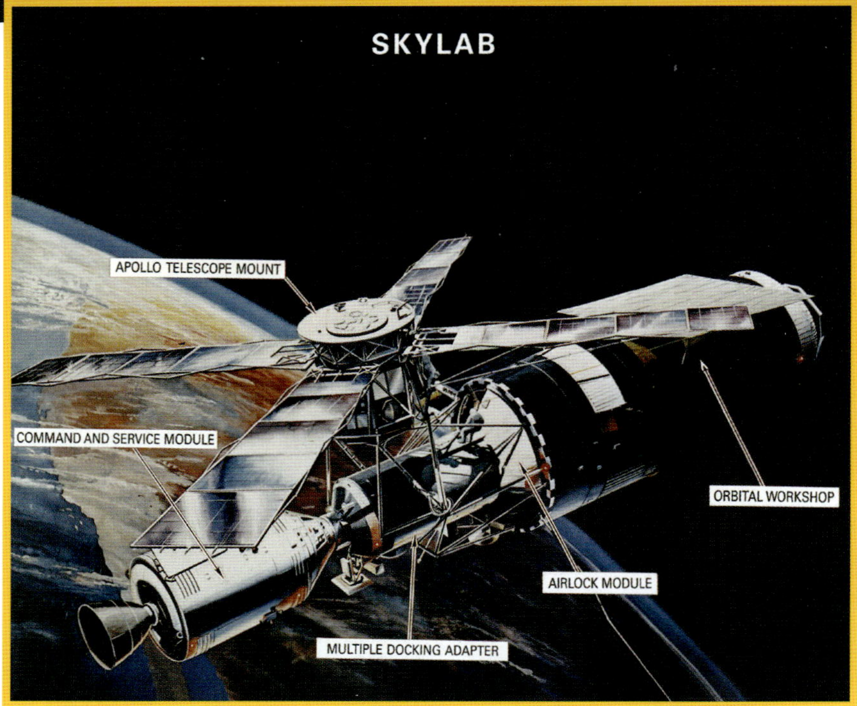

This illustration shows the various components of Skylab. Pieces of the space station were recovered from remote areas of Australia and are on display at the US Space and Rocket Center in Huntsville, Alabama.

Apollo-Soyuz

The final Apollo mission resulted from an agreement between US President Richard Nixon and Soviet Premier Aleksey Kosygin. In what was to be called the Apollo-Soyuz Test Project, the two previously bitter rivals joined forces to design and build two spacecraft—an American Apollo and a Soviet Soyuz—to rendezvous in Earth orbit. They would link up using a common docking module located between the two spacecraft.

While the Apollo-Soyuz Test Project was largely a program of political propaganda meant to show that two longtime rivals in the space race could cooperate peacefully, it did accomplish several scientific goals; the most important was a common docking system that allowed two different spacecraft from two different countries to link up in orbit. The techniques and lessons learned could be applied to future collaborative efforts in space exploration.

To make sure that everything would go smoothly, Russian cosmonauts

Alexei Leonov (who had made the first space walk several years earlier) and Valery Kubasov underwent training at Johnson Space Center in Texas. Meanwhile, American astronauts Stafford, Vance Brand, and Slayton traveled to Moscow to train there.

Launched on July 15, 1975, the two spacecraft rendezvoused and docked two days later, with Leonov and Stafford exchanging the first international handshake in space as they met in the hatch connecting the spacecraft. After exchanging gifts, the two teams practiced docking and redocking.

The international cooperation that led to the success of the Apollo-Soyuz Test Project paved the way for the collaboration that resulted in the International Space Station.

Artificial Gravity Experiment

This experiment is best performed in a classroom or outdoors. You will need the following:

- **string**
- **a paper cup**
- **jelly beans (or any small, round objects)**

Attach a loop of string to the rim of a small paper cup. Then tie a string about 4 feet (1.2 m) long to the loop. Place a few jelly beans in the cup. Taking the other end of the string in your hand, whirl the cup around your head in a circular motion.

Why don't the jelly beans fall out of the cup? They are held in place by centrifugal force. They are trying to fly away from your hand in a straight line, but the bottom of the cup keeps them from doing that. Instead, they are held against the bottom of the cup.

The bottom of the cup stands in for the floor of a rotating space station, and the jelly beans are the astronauts aboard. As the station rotates around its center, the astronauts are held to the floor by centrifugal force. If the space station rotates at just the right speed, the force will feel the same as gravity on Earth.

The International Space Station

In 1984 President Reagan gave the go-ahead to construct an orbiting space station. But such a large project could not be undertaken by one country by itself. The cost alone would be immense. Building and maintaining a large space station for ten years cost more than $100 billion, nearly four times the cost of the entire Apollo program. To help share the cost and effort in developing and building a large space station, NASA invited space agencies in Canada, Europe, and Japan to take part in the project. Five space agencies representing fifteen countries participated in building and maintaining the station as well as providing crew members. These agencies included the

Living in Weightlessness

One of the concerns scientists and doctors had in the early days of space travel was the effect prolonged weightlessness would have on the human body. This was an important consideration for future long-term space missions, such as those to Mars, which would require more than half a year just to make the trip to the planet. The biggest worry was that bones would lose the calcium that makes them strong and lead to extra calcium in an astronaut's bloodstream. The extra calcium might lead to the formation of painful—and potentially dangerous—kidney stones. Muscles—including the heart—would also grow weaker the longer a person remained in space. In addition to the concerns about microgravity, a state of near weightlessness, doctors worried about the effects of long exposure to radiation.

While spaceflights such as the Apollo missions provided a great deal of useful information about the effects of long-term spaceflight of days or weeks, Mir and the International Space Station gave astronauts a chance to experience weightlessness for months. Between January 1994 and March 1995, Russian cosmonaut Valeri Polyakov spent a record 437 days in orbit aboard Russia's Mir space station. American astronaut Frank Rubio spent 371 days aboard the International Space Station in 2022 and 2023. While both suffered some of the expected ill effects of long exposure to weightlessness, exercise and other preventive measures helped keep the men relatively healthy.

Canadian Space Agency, the European Space Agency, the Japan Aerospace Exploration Agency, and the Russian space agency, Roscosmos.

Russia launched the first module of the future space station on November 20, 1998. It consisted of the batteries, fuel storage, and docking capabilities needed to support the modules yet to come. Two weeks later, on December 4, the United States launched its first space station module.

All of the participating countries eventually contributed materials and personnel to the growing International Space Station (ISS). Each country was responsible for maintaining whatever components of the ISS it provided. Building the ISS required thirty-seven space shuttle flights and the launches of five Russian spacecraft over ten years. The space station has been continuously occupied since November 2000, with a crew of between three and thirteen people. When the first ISS crew arrived on November 2, 2000, the station consisted of just three modules. Since then, ISS has grown to the size of a football field with sixteen pressurized modules. More than 260 astronauts and scientists from twenty-one countries have worked there. Since the retirement of the Space Shuttle program in 2011, personnel and supplies have been carried to the ISS by Russian Progress and Soyuz spacecraft, the Japanese H-II Transfer Vehicle, the European Space Agency's Automated Transfer Vehicle, and the Dragon, Cygnus, and Starliner vehicles operated by private businesses.

The ISS is the largest object ever placed in orbit by humans. It is larger than a six-bedroom house, with six sleeping quarters, two bathrooms, a gym, and a dome-shaped window providing a 360-degree view of Earth. The ISS is 356 feet (110 m) from end to end and weighs more than 900,000 pounds (408,000 kg). The solar panel arrays alone extend more than half an acre (24,187 sq. feet, or 2,247 sq. m). Eight spacecraft can dock at the ISS at once, and its international crew lives and works aboard while traveling at a speed of 5 miles (8 km) per second, completing a full orbit around Earth every ninety minutes.

Scientists in Space

The ISS has contributed a great deal to space science. Over its ninety-minute orbit, the ISS crosses over 90 percent of Earth's populated regions. Astronauts

Astronauts aboard the ISS have shared photographs they take of Earth on social media.

aboard have taken millions of images of the planet below. These photos have helped scientists understand the effects of farming, industry, forestry, climate change, weather and ocean current patterns, soil erosion, air pollution, and many other changes.

The research conducted on the ISS has also benefited other fields, including medicine and public health. Scientists working aboard the station have developed new, more efficient ways of filtering air and water. NASA's development of new X-ray machines has led to improvements to medical scanning technology that reduce patients' exposure to radiation. New drugs with the potential to treat muscular dystrophy, a disease that causes one's muscles to weaken and lose mass, have been developed by ISS scientists. A robotic glove invented to help ISS astronauts perform tasks has been adapted for use by workers on Earth to reduce hand fatigue and injury. A miniaturized ultrasound device developed to enable astronauts to easily examine one another has allowed doctors in underdeveloped countries to diagnose patients quickly and safely.

There have also been direct benefits to the well-being of people on Earth. This is largely due to the unique environment in which the space station operates. Scientists can work with materials in microgravity because the mass of the space station has a minute effect on gravity. They can work with molecules that would be difficult or impossible to create on Earth's surface. The ISS microgravity laboratory has hosted more than three thousand research projects of scientists from more than 108 countries.

Crystals, molecules, and living cells grow differently in microgravity. Not being confined to a flat plane by gravity, they develop in a more three-dimensional way. This sometimes makes them easier to study. For example, protein molecules are very large and complex, making them tricky to synthesize in a laboratory. But the lack of gravity at the ISS makes the molecules less fragile. They grow larger and are easier to create. This has led to new medical treatments and a greater understanding of many illnesses. Scientists aboard the ISS have studied the structure of protein molecules associated with Parkinson's disease, enabling them to develop better ways of detecting and controlling the disease, which disables or kills nearly nine million people around the world every year. More than five hundred experiments in protein crystal growth have been performed by scientists on the ISS, more than any other type of research.

An experimental success occurred when chile pepper plants aboard the ISS bore fruit. Growing fruit and vegetables in space instead of bringing them from Earth helps astronauts stay healthy while reducing the weight of the rocket at launch.

The End of the ISS

The ISS was never meant to be permanent. Its orbit at 250 miles (402 km) above the surface of Earth is just low enough that the atmosphere—nearly as thin as a vacuum at that altitude—has a cumulative effect on the station's orbit, gradually slowing it down. When the station moves more slowly, its orbit becomes lower. Every now and then, astronauts fire rocket thrusters to nudge the ISS back up to its proper orbit. The ISS also experiences stress from the constantly changing temperature as it moves from the sunlit side of Earth into the planet's shadow. NASA decided that the ISS would last no longer than the year 2030.

The physical wear and tear on the ISS was only part of that decision. Political friction between Russia and the other participating nations led Russia to threaten to leave the ISS in 2024. That would be catastrophic to the station's operations. Russia operates six of the seventeen modules as well as the station's propulsion system: the thrusters that are used to maintain its orbit. And of all the participating nations, only Russia has the resources, launch vehicles, and funding to keep the space station fully operational.

Meanwhile, NASA has been working toward supporting commercial space stations—stations built and maintained by private companies. At the end of 2021, NASA awarded Blue Origin and two other companies more than $415 million to develop their own space station designs. NASA had already been using private spacecraft to transport crews and supplies to the ISS. By turning over space station construction and maintenance to private companies, NASA can devote its funds and facilities to new projects.

One of the biggest questions in decommissioning the ISS is, Where will it come down? The station is huge, so some of its largest components will likely reach the ground before they completely burn up in the atmosphere. If they do, they could cause damage or even casualties. When Skylab, which was much smaller than the ISS, fell back into Earth's atmosphere most of it burned up—but some pieces survived long enough to reach the ground. NASA plans to carefully orchestrate the fall of the ISS so that it will disintegrate over a remote area of the Pacific Ocean, a point farthest removed from all land.

Chapter 7

Exploring the Inner Solar System

While NASA was sending human explorers into space and landing astronauts on the moon, it had not been ignoring the other worlds in the solar system.

It was only natural that Earth's moon came first. Just as the Soviet Union had beaten the United States into space with Sputnik 1, it was also the first to send spacecraft to the moon. The Soviet Luna 1 flew past the moon in January 1959. Later, Luna 3 photographed the far side of the moon, which is never visible from Earth, and humans saw what the far side looked like for the first time. (The same side of the moon always faces our planet.) It was covered in craters of every size and age, and did not have the darker regions that we see on the near side.

Americans felt a patriotic urge to catch up with the Soviets, but after President Kennedy announced in 1961 the plan to send an American to the moon, there were more reasons to send spacecraft to the moon. If humans were to land there safely, they needed to find out exactly what the moon was like. Was the surface solid rock, or was it, as many scientists suspected, covered in a deep layer of dust? Was the layer so deep that a lander might sink into it?

Pioneer and Ranger

The first of the American probes to the moon was the Pioneer series launched in 1958. None of the four spacecraft succeeded in its planned mission. Three failed to achieve sufficient speed to reach the moon, and another failed to come close enough to gather any data. NASA followed these up with the Ranger program. The Ranger spacecraft were large—between 700 and 800 pounds (317 to 363 kg)—and each was equipped with solar panels to power its radio, scientific instruments, and six television cameras. The plan was to photograph the surface of the moon from a range of distances, starting at about 870 miles (1,400 km) and getting as close as half a mile (0.8 km), as the spacecraft plummeted toward it. NASA launched nine Rangers between 1961 and 1965. The first to successfully reach the moon, Ranger 4, crashed into the surface as planned but failed to transmit any information back to Earth. Ranger 7, launched on July 29, 1964, sent 4,316 images back to Earth, and Rangers 8 and 9 returned a total of 12,951 images of the lunar surface. These enabled scientists to get their first close-up look at the surface of the moon—especially regions in the Sea of Tranquility, the Sea of Clouds, and the crater Alphonsus, the three locations where NASA planned on doing human landings.

Meanwhile, in 1960, NASA received approval from Congress to develop its Surveyor program. Originally, Surveyor would consist of an orbiter that would circle the moon, taking pictures and gathering data, and a lander that would detach and set down on the surface. The project's limited budget resulted in the orbiting component of Surveyor being split into a separate program: the Lunar Orbiter.

Lunar Orbiter

The Lunar Orbiter spacecraft weighed 853 pounds (387 kg) and had two main parts: a small rocket engine with fuel tanks and a platform carrying the scientific instruments and television camera the orbiter used to collect data. Attached to the platform were four solar panels that provided power to the spacecraft.

Lunar Orbiter 1 was a success. Launched on August 10, 1966, it sent 207 images of the moon back to Earth before impacting in October that year. The images focused on potential Apollo landing sites.

Lunar Orbiter 1 was followed by four more Lunar Orbiter missions. Like Lunar Orbiter 1, they took close-up photos of possible landing sites for the Apollo astronauts as well as landing sites for the Surveyor landers. Although the orbiters returned only a few hundred images, compared to the thousands from Ranger, these were of much higher quality, allowing scientists to get a more accurate idea about what the surface of the moon was like. The orbiters also returned photos of areas on the moon normally difficult or impossible to see from Earth, such as the lunar southern polar regions and the far side.

Surveyor

Surveyor would be the first spacecraft to land on the moon—rather than crash into it, Surveyor was designed to remain intact. Of the seven Surveyor spacecraft launched to the moon, five landed successfully. Surveyor 1, launched on May 30, 1966, set down on the moon on June 2. It sent

Astronaut Alan Bean visits Surveyor 3. In the background of the photograph taken by Pete Conrad is the Lunar Module from their Apollo 12 mission.

back ten thousand images of the lunar surface before shutting down the following January. These were the first photos taken on the surface of the moon.

Surveyor 2 failed, but Surveyor 3 made a successful landing in April 1967. In addition to sending more than six thousand images back to Earth, it gathered information about the moon's surface. It was equipped with an extendable sampler arm that dug a trench in the lunar soil. Close-up photos of the trench and the samples told scientists a great deal about the composition and strength of the lunar surface—important data for a future human landing.

Two Apollo 12 astronauts, Pete Conrad and Alan Bean, landed within walking distance of Surveyor 3 and visited it in November 1969.

Surveyor 4 failed, but the last three spacecraft in the series were successful, returning not only photos but also valuable information about the chemical composition of the lunar surface.

The Moon Since Apollo

NASA more or less ignored the moon following the Apollo landings. The next spacecraft, Clementine, that went to Earth's neighbor was not launched until January 25, 1994. It reached and began orbiting the moon twenty-four days later. Circling the moon 297 times, it sent 1.6 million high-resolution digital images of the moon back to Earth. Objects as small as 330 feet (100 m) across were visible. For the first time, scientists had detailed images of the entire lunar surface, including the polar regions.

One of the most important discoveries made by Clementine was evidence of ice in the bottom of a crater at the lunar south pole that, due to the depth of the crater, is permanently shaded from the sun. If the presence of ice is confirmed, this would be of immense value to the creation of future inhabited lunar bases. The ice would not only be a source of water but of oxygen and even rocket fuel.

Clementine's original mission was not only to study the moon but also a nearby asteroid. Once Clementine finished photographing the lunar surface, it would be launched out of its orbit toward an asteroid known as 1620 Geographos. If it succeeded, it would have been the first spacecraft to visit an asteroid. But a booster failure forced NASA to abandon the idea.

NASA sent two more spacecraft to the moon in 2009. The Lunar Reconnaissance Orbiter created the first 3D maps of the moon and also found evidence of ice. The orbiter was launched with the Lunar Crater Observation and Sensing Satellite to determine if water ice (frozen water) exists in a permanently shadowed crater at the moon's south pole, such as the one Clementine discovered. To do this, NASA crashed it into a crater near the south pole. Observing the plume of material that rose above the impact, scientists found that the lunar soil is rich in useful minerals and confirmed the existence of pure water ice on the moon. These resources could be collected and used by astronauts in future missions.

On September 10, 2011, NASA launched the Gravity Recovery and Interior Laboratory to the moon, a pair of spacecraft whose mission was to study variations in the moon's gravitational field. Variations in gravity can give scientists information about the interior structure of the moon. The names of the two spacecraft, Ebb and Flow, were the result of a national contest won by the fourth-grade students at Emily Dickinson Elementary School in Bozeman, Montana.

The most recent NASA mission to the moon is the Lunar Atmosphere and Dust Environment Explorer spacecraft. It was the first deep space mission to be launched from NASA's Wallops Flight Facility in Virginia. Established by NACA in 1945, it is the nation's oldest continuously operating rocket launch facility.

This spacecraft was designed to answer questions about the origins and features of the ice on the moon. Where did the ice come from, how long had it been there, and how long would it last? To get closer to the answers, scientists needed to know more about the environment. Arriving on September 7, 2013, this spacecraft orbited the moon for one hundred days. It was eventually impacted onto the surface, gathering information about the lunar atmosphere, conditions near the surface, and the environmental influences on lunar dust.

Although the moon is famously airless, it has an atmosphere of sorts, although so thin as to be almost indistinguishable from a vacuum. This atmosphere consists of helium, argon, neon, ammonia, methane, and carbon dioxide. One reason for the very thin atmosphere is the moon's low gravity—only a sixth that of Earth's. It has a hard time holding onto light gases. Heated by the sun, the gases on the moon boil away into space like water evaporating from a puddle.

In the past decade, NASA has had several other missions to the moon. The first was Artemis. Rather than build entirely new spacecraft, NASA repurposed a couple of probes that were originally part of a mission called THEMIS that had been orbiting Earth since 2007 to study auroras. Since auroras are created by the solar wind interacting with Earth's atmosphere, measuring them provides valuable information about solar storms, powerful emissions from the sun that can cause power outages and disrupt satellite communications. Analyzing auroras can also tell scientists much about the conditions and composition of Earth's upper atmosphere. THEMIS consisted of five satellites, A, B, C, D, and E. When that mission had been completed, NASA renamed probes B and C to Artemis P1 and P2 and sent them to the moon in 2009.

Among the ten smaller lunar satellites launched along with a new spacecraft, Artemis 1, in November 2022, were LunaH-Map and Lunar IceCube. Both were tasked with finding water ice on the moon's surface.

Another in the set was Cislunar Autonomous Positioning System Technology Operations and Navigation Experiment, an orbiter meant to pave the way for the Gateway space station. Gateway will be the first human-occupied space station to circle another world. It will be both a research facility and a halfway point for astronauts traveling to and from the surface of the moon. Like the International Space Station, Gateway will be an international project led by NASA.

The Sun

NASA has not ignored the center of our solar system, our sun. Of all the bodies in the solar system, the sun has the most impact on our planet. The amount of radiation Earth receives from the sun—in light, heat, and the solar wind—has both positive and negative effects, depending on how much energy the sun is emitting at any one time. Bursts in the solar wind can interfere with electronics in satellites and even interfere with electronics and communication on Earth. The sun is also the only star that we can study up close (the next closest star is 4.2 light-years, or about 25 trillion

CubeSat

LunaH-Map, Lunar IceCube, and Cislunar Autonomous Positioning System Technology Operations and Navigation Experiment are all examples of a type of small satellite called a CubeSat. These are made to a standard size and configuration. They are built from a standard cube measuring about 4 inches (10 cm) on each side. CubeSats can be constructed of one cube or in combinations up to twelve, in much the same way Lego blocks can be assembled. The typical CubeSat weighs only between 2 and 20 pounds (0.9 to 9 kg). NASA launched its first CubeSat, GeneSat, in December 2006.

miles [40 trillion km], away), so what we learn about it informs us about other stars in the universe.

Through a fleet of nineteen active orbiting solar observatories, NASA keeps an eye on the sun twenty-four hours a day.

The Orbiting Solar Observatory was the first of eight similar satellites launched between 1962 and 1975. The last one operated until 1978. The sun's activity follows an eleven-year cycle. During the period of greatest activity, the number of sunspots on the sun's surface peaks, and when its activity is at the lowest, so is the number of sunspots. The Orbiting Solar Observatory satellites were designed to study the sun through one of these cycles.

NASA manages many active solar observatories, including the Solar and Heliospheric Observatory, the Advanced Composition Explorer, the Interface Region Imaging Spectrograph, Wind, Hinode, the Solar Dynamics Observatory, and the Solar Terrestrial Relations Observatory. All are designed to study different features of our star. The Advanced Composition Explorer gathered particles of the solar wind for study, and Hinode studies the sun's magnetic field, while the Solar Terrestrial Relations Observatory has two spacecraft that provided 3D images of solar phenomenon, such as coronal mass ejections, spectacular bubblelike explosions on the sun's surface that launch magnetic fields and billions of tons of matter outward at speeds of millions of miles an hour. When the outburst reaches Earth, it can cause serious disruptions in communications, electronics, and electrical

This diagram made from data from NASA's Solar Dynamics Observatory shows magnetic field lines plotted over an ultraviolet image of the sun. A higher concentration of lines indicates more magnetic activity.

grids. On March 13, 1989, a coronal mass ejection caused a major power blackout in Canada that left six million people without electricity for nine hours. Events such as this underscore the importance of studying the sun and understanding how it works.

One of the most recent spacecraft to study the sun is NASA's Parker Solar Probe. Its mission is to map the flow of energy within the sun, study how the sun's corona—its outer atmosphere—is heated, and determine what accelerates solar wind. Since all of these things have a direct effect on our planet, Parker will enable scientists to better understand the relationship between the sun and Earth.

In December 2021, the probe flew through the sun's corona. This took it within 4 million miles (6.4 million km) of the sun, ten times closer than the planet Mercury. It was the first time that a spacecraft had actually touched the sun. Parker will orbit around the sun twenty-four times before its mission is complete. A shield 4.5 inches (11 cm) thick protects the spacecraft from temperatures as high as 2,500°F (1,371°C).

Venus

Often called Earth's twin because it resembles our planet so closely in size, our planetary neighbor Venus had always been a mystery. Because Venus is covered from pole to pole by dense clouds, no astronomer had ever gotten a glimpse of the surface. No one knew what the conditions might be there. Some thought the planet might be a vast jungle, perhaps resembling Earth during the time of the dinosaurs. Others thought it might be entirely covered by an ocean, or it might be a vast desert.

To help solve the many mysteries about Earth's twin, NASA initiated the Mariner program. The first attempt, Mariner 1, failed at takeoff. A month later, on August 27, 1962, Mariner 2 was sent on its way to Venus. It arrived in December 1962, becoming the first spacecraft to reach another planet. It was not designed to either land on Venus, or even to orbit it, which would have required a much more complex mission. Instead, it flew within 20,000 miles (32,187 km) of the planet. Instruments aboard measured the temperature of the surface of Venus, gathered information about the composition of the planet's atmosphere, and discovered that Venus, unlike Earth, might have no magnetic field. It also found that the scientists who had predicted that Venus was a desert world had been underestimating the planet. Mariner 2 found surface temperatures of 421°F (216°C) on the night side (facing away from the sun) and 459°F (237°C) on the day side (facing toward the sun), temperatures hot enough to melt tin. After flying past Venus, Mariner 2 eventually fell into orbit around the sun.

NASA launched Pioneer Venus 1 on May 20, 1978. Arriving on December 4, it became the first spacecraft to orbit the planet. Using radar—which can differentiate between rough and smooth surfaces—the spacecraft was able to map nearly 93 percent of the surface of Venus. The highest point it found, Maxwell Montes, rose 6.5 miles (10.5 km) above the surrounding surface, higher than Mount Everest, Earth's highest mountain. Cameras aboard the spacecraft sent the first close-up images of Venus back to Earth while other instruments confirmed the planet's lack of a magnetic field.

Over a decade later, NASA again visited Venus. The Magellan probe—launched on May 4, 1989, from the space shuttle Atlantis—used radar to map nearly 100 percent of the surface to a resolution of 390 to 985 feet

(120 to 300 m). Details smaller than 400 feet (122 m) wide were imaged. At least 85 percent of the surface of Venus is covered with volcanic flows. Magellan also confirmed the high surface temperature suggested by Mariner 2, discovering that it was even higher at 887°F (475°C). This is hot enough to melt not just tin but lead and zinc. The pressure of Venus's atmosphere at the surface was found to be a crushing ninety-two times that of the atmosphere at the surface of Earth. The pressure of the air on you as you read this is 14 pounds per square inch (1 kg per sq. cm). On Venus it is 1,350 pounds per square inch (95 kg per sq. cm)—more than half a ton (0.5 t). One reason for such a heavy atmosphere is its composition: It is mostly CO_2, a gas that is about 150 percent heavier than Earth's air, which is made mostly of oxygen and nitrogen.

Mars

Mars had lured the attention of astronomers and scientists since the end of the nineteenth century. The planet had long been known to have Earthlike qualities: an atmosphere with clouds, dusky markings on its surface, and even bright white polar caps. Of the bodies in the solar system that might be a potential abode for life, Mars was certainly a prime candidate.

The first flyby of Mars was accomplished by NASA's Mariner 4 spacecraft. It was one of ten Mariner spacecraft, which were meant to explore Mercury, Venus, and Mars. Mariner 3 failed to launch properly, but on November 28, 1964, Mariner 4 was sent on its way to the red planet. The spacecraft flew past Mars on July 14, 1965, collecting the first close-up photographs of another planet's surface. The images surprised the scientists who saw them because they revealed a crater-covered world that seemed to resemble our own moon. Mariners 6 and 7, flying by Mars in 1968, snapped more photos that confirmed the craters. Mariner 9 was the last of the Mariner series to reach Mars. Unlike its predecessors, it did not fly past the planet. Instead, it went into orbit.

To the disappointment of the scientists watching images arrive from the spacecraft's cameras, the planet was covered almost entirely, pole to pole, by a vast dust storm. The surface was invisible. They had to wait until the dust settled, which took nearly a month.

The planet looked very different from the moonlike world the previous Mariners had suggested. As the dust cleared, three large dark spots became visible: huge craters at the summits of mountains. Scientists realized that the mountains were enormous volcanoes, the largest in the solar system. A vast canyon stretched 3,000 miles (4,828 km) across Mars's surface—as long as the width of the continental United States. The biggest surprise was evidence of ancient riverbeds, a sign that Mars once had water flowing on its surface.

Mariner 9 even took snapshots of Mars's two little moons, Phobos and Deimos: the first time astronomers had ever gotten a close-up view of another planet's moons.

NASA's next missions to Mars were more ambitious. On July 20 and September 3, 1976, two probes, Viking 1 and 2, arrived at Mars after journeys of nearly a year. Both spacecraft had two parts: an orbiter and a lander.

The landers conducted three biology experiments designed to look for signs of life on Mars. To scientists' surprise, the landers detected some chemical activity in the soil that could have been produced by living organisms. But there were other possible explanations, so they could not be certain.

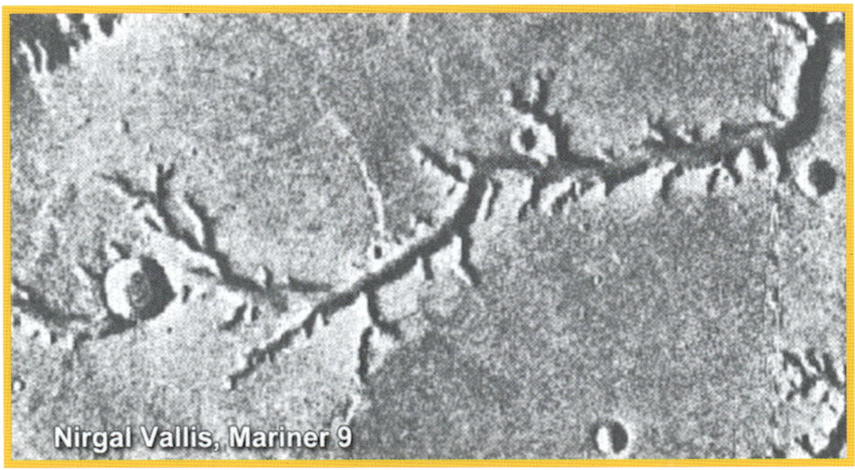

Mariner 9 took many images of the surface of Mars that show features similar to those found on Earth. This feature resembles a river, leading scientists to believe Mars has or once had water flowing on its surface.

Scientists had two reasons for doubting that the landers had discovered life. One is that Mars was believed to be extremely dry, having lost almost all of its surface water millions of years ago. Another is that its very thin atmosphere doesn't shield the surface from ultraviolet radiation from the sun, as Earth's atmosphere does. Life as we know it cannot survive without water and cannot withstand the blasts of radiation that the surface of Mars experiences. The combination, scientists believed, sterilized the surface of Mars—it could not sustain life.

After performing the biology experiment, the Viking landers took photos of the surrounding landscape and gathered data about conditions on the surface. Perhaps the biggest surprise was the color of the Martian sky. It was pink! For more than a century, astronomers had assumed that the sky of Mars would be dark blue, like the sky on Earth when seen from a very high altitude, where the air is thin. But the atmosphere of Mars is filled with fine dust lifted from the surface by wind and dust storms. This dust has turned the sky pink.

The Viking mission was designed to operate for only three months, but surprisingly Viking Orbiter 1 continued for another four years, until 1980, after orbiting Mars 1,489 times, and Viking Orbiter 2 operated until 1978. Meanwhile, Viking Lander 1 made its final transmission to Earth in 1982, and Viking Lander 2 did so in 1980.

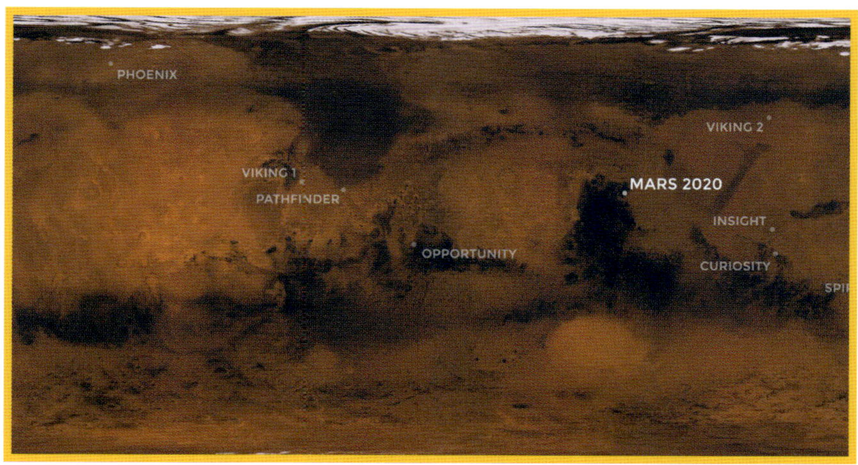

NASA has sent landers and rovers all across the surface of Mars, but many regions are still completely unexplored.

The Pathfinder mission of 1997 took the next step and set a robotic rover onto the surface of Mars. Pathfinder's landing was unique. As the lander, containing the rover, descended into the Martian atmosphere, it released a parachute to slow itself down. As it neared the surface, it inflated a cluster of twenty-four airbags around the spacecraft, which then dropped free from the parachute. The airbag-protected lander hit the surface of Mars, bouncing across the landscape like a huge beach ball. Once it came to rest, the airbags deflated, and the lander opened to allow the rover to roll away. The rover was named Sojourner, a name suggested by Valerie Ambroise, a twelve-year-old student in Connecticut, who was inspired by Sojourner Truth, an African American abolitionist who worked during the Civil War to help end the enslavement of Black people in the United States. The lander was named the Carl Sagan station, after the famous astronomer and science popularizer.

The lander was equipped with cameras and sent 16,500 images back to Earth. Meanwhile, Sojourner sent 550 images along with the results of fifteen chemical experiments performed on rocks and soil. It also sent information about temperature, wind, and weather. Photos showed wispy clouds of ice high in the sky and dust devils—like little tornadoes—spinning across the surface.

From this data, scientists concluded that in the distant past, Mars had been warm and wet. Perhaps warm and wet enough for life to have evolved. Some small pebbles Sojourner examined could only have formed in running water, suggesting that Mars once had rivers, confirming the evidence suggested by photos taken by Mariner 9 more than twenty years earlier.

The next mission to Mars was an orbiter. The instruments and cameras aboard the Mars Global Surveyor, which operated from 1997 to 2006, revealed that the weather on Mars, like that of Earth, followed regular patterns. It also confirmed that liquid water once existed at or near the surface.

Excited by Sojourner and the Mars Global Surveyor's invaluable findings, NASA planned many more missions to Mars to look for evidence of water and life, past or present. It landed two more rovers on Mars in 2004. The rovers, Spirit and Opportunity, were much larger and more capable than the little Sojourner, which was only 2 feet (63 cm) long and weighed just 23 pounds (10.6 kg). The twin rovers stood 5 feet (1.5 m) tall, were 5.2 feet (1.6 m) long, and weighed 400 pounds (180 kg).

During their mission, the rovers returned hundreds of thousands of full-color, high-resolution photos. They conducted hundreds of experiments on Martian rocks and soil, discovering that Mars had been much wetter in the past than previous data suggested—that it might have had rivers, lakes, and even seas—and that conditions might once have been ideal for microbial life. Like the Viking landers, Spirit and Opportunity exceeded their expected mission life of ninety days. Spirit worked until 2010, and Opportunity continued to operate for fifteen years after it landed.

Mars Phoenix landed near the Martian north pole in 2008. Its primary goal during its six-month mission was to look for water ice at or near the surface of the planet. One of the tools the lander used was a robotic arm that could dig up to 7 inches (18 cm) into the ground, gathering samples that were analyzed by a miniature laboratory inside the lander. Phoenix confirmed the existence of water ice as well as a chemical called perchlorate, a source of energy for some microbial life on Earth. While good news for any microbes that might be living on Mars, perchlorates are toxic to human beings. Since perchlorate can be a source of oxygen and is an ingredient in many solid rocket fuels, it may be useful to future explorers.

Landing on Mars in November 2018, InSight was the first probe to record earthquakes—or Marsquakes—on the planet, using a seismometer, an instrument that measures vibrations in the ground. It has recorded more than thirteen hundred tremors, many of them originating from the locations of ancient volcanoes. Since earthquake waves travel through the deepest layers of the planet and are affected by the density of different materials, they give scientists a view similar to an X-ray of the interior of Mars.

Continuing the search for signs of life, the Perseverance rover set down on Mars on February 18, 2021, and began to collect samples of rock and soil for a future spacecraft to bring back to Earth. It also carried something very unusual: a little helicopter called Ingenuity, the first aircraft to be flown on another planet. Weighing only 4 pounds (1.8 kg) and standing at 19 inches (48 cm) high, Ingenuity looks like a toy, but like other NASA spacecraft, it exceeded expectations. Originally planned to make only five test flights over thirty days, it performed for more than three years since it first took off from Perseverance on April 29, 2021. Equipped with a camera, it took hundreds of photos of the terrain surrounding the Perseverance landing site, reaching areas that would have been difficult or even impossible for the rover to visit. After making its seventy-second flight on January 18, 2024, Ingenuity broke one of its rotor blades during a landing. The little helicopter was permanently grounded.

Mercury

Mariner 10, launched on November 3, 1973, reached the innermost planet of the solar system, Mercury, on March 29, 1974, with a gravitation assist from Venus. It was the first spacecraft to use the gravitation assist from one planet to reach another. When two bodies in space encounter each other, such as a spacecraft and a planet, one loses energy and the other gains energy. Why not, scientists asked, have the spacecraft fly by Venus at exactly the right distance and angle so that it gains energy from the planet's gravity? Its speed would be increased, and the direction it was traveling could be changed. With the right calculations and precise aim, scientists could send spacecraft to farther destinations faster and save on fuel. The success of Mariner 10's gravitation assist inspired NASA to use the method for many more spacecraft.

Mariner 10 added several more firsts to its list of accomplishments. It was the first spacecraft to visit two planets: Venus and then Mercury. After its first encounter with Mercury, Mariner 10 circled the sun and returned for a second flyby—another first. The spacecraft was also able to take a close look at a comet, C/1973 E1, or Kohoutek. Astronauts aboard the Skylab space station were simultaneously observing the comet.

Mariner made three flybys of Mercury and returned over twenty-seven hundred pictures. These revealed a rugged moonlike world covered in craters. Details as small as 328 feet (100 m) wide can be seen in some of the images. The most impressive feature it found is probably Caloris basin. Created by the impact of a giant asteroid millions of years ago, the crater has concentric rings and ridges that look like a huge bull's-eye 1,550 miles (2,500 km) wide. It was given the name Caloris from the Latin word for "heat" since Mercury is the planet closest to the sun.

Chapter 8

Exploring the Outer Solar System

The outer planets of the solar system are so much farther away than Mars that they seemed beyond our reach. Maybe we could send a probe to Jupiter, some at NASA thought, but Saturn, Uranus, Neptune and, especially, Pluto were much farther away. Jupiter is four times farther away from the sun than Earth is—less than twice the distance of Mars. But Saturn in more than nine times farther away and Pluto a boggling thirty-nine times farther.

Scientists needed to figure out a way to give spacecraft an extra boost in speed, so they decided to use the technique of gravitational assist that had worked so well with Mariner 10 on its mission to Mercury. The spacecraft would get an increase in speed and a change in direction from the giant planet Jupiter.

The perfect time for trying out this technique would occur in the late 1970s. All of the outer planets would be lined up in such a way that a single spacecraft, if launched exactly the right way, would be able to encounter three or four planets instead of one. The gravity of each planet would give the spacecraft a boost toward the next. NASA called this plan for hopping from one planet to another the Grand Tour.

For this to work, NASA scientists needed to know more about Jupiter and the conditions a spacecraft might encounter on its journey to the gas giant. One barrier a spacecraft would have to cross would be the asteroid belt, a region of rocky and metallic bodies—ranging in size from backyard rocks to mountains—orbiting between Mars and Jupiter and separating the inner and outer planets. While the orbits of the biggest asteroids were well known, the belt might be so full of small, nearly invisible debris that it would pose a danger to any spacecraft passing through it. Even if the spacecraft made it through the asteroid belt without any trouble, scientists also knew Jupiter had a powerful magnetic field trapping solar radiation, surrounding the planet with a kind of shield that would damage a spacecraft's delicate electronic instruments if it got too close. They needed to measure Jupiter's radiation to get a clearer picture of the risks, or else the Grand Tour could come to an early end.

Pioneer to Jupiter and Saturn

NASA launched the Pioneer Project to help answer some of these questions. The Pioneer 10 and 11 spacecraft were part of the same family that had visited Venus. Like the other Pioneers, 10 and 11 were small: about the size of a kitchen range and weighing only about 570 pounds (258 kg). Since they would travel too far from the sun for solar panels to work, they were equipped with nuclear power generators that used the heat produced by radioactive plutonium to create electricity.

Pioneer 10 was launched on March 2, 1972, on a mission to fly by the planet Jupiter. Nineteen months later, it flew past Jupiter at a distance of 81,000 miles (130,357 km), capturing the first close-up images of the giant planet. Halfway through its journey, it became the first spacecraft to travel through the asteroid belt. Scientists were relieved to find that the density of objects in the belt that could damage the spacecraft was much lower than expected. In addition to taking photos of Jupiter and several of its moons, Pioneer 10 also transmitted information about Jupiter's atmosphere and measured the magnetic field and belts of radiation that surround the planet.

Long after its encounter with Jupiter, Pioneer 10 continued to transmit data about the outer solar system until its mission was officially ended in March 1997. Amazingly, scientists could still detect a faint signal from the spacecraft until 2003. By 2024, Pioneer 10 was more than 12 billion miles (19.3 billion km) from Earth, nearly 134 times farther away from the sun than Earth is. From the little spacecraft, the sun is nearly 18,000 times dimmer than it appears in our skies.

Pioneer 11, launched on April 6, 1973, flew by Jupiter in 1974, approaching within 26,718 miles (43,000 km). It was able to not only record even more information about Jupiter and its radiation belts but take much more detailed images of the planet.

Using information gathered from Pioneer 10's encounter with Jupiter, Pioneer 11's trajectory was carefully adjusted so that when it swung past Jupiter, the planet's gravity increased the spacecraft's speed and changed its direction toward Saturn, which was on the opposite side of the sun from Jupiter. The spacecraft was renamed Pioneer Saturn as it continued on to the ringed planet.

As it flew by Saturn five years later, Pioneer took 440 images, many of them revealing details as small as 56 miles (90 km) wide. It also returned fascinating photos of Saturn's largest moon, Titan, which looked like a fuzzy orange tennis ball, indicating that the moon had a dense atmosphere entirely covered by clouds. Pioneer's images also revealed new rings circling the planet that were too faint to be seen from Earth.

With the completion of the two Pioneer flybys of Jupiter and a successful gravitation assist to Saturn, NASA was ready to send larger, more complex spacecraft on a Grand Tour to the outer planets.

The Grand Tour

The spacecraft that conducted the Grand Tour are among the most famous in NASA's history: Voyager 1 and Voyager 2. The original plan for the twin spacecraft was to perform flybys of Jupiter and Saturn as well as Saturn's rings and make close encounters with as many of those planets' moons as possible.

Voyager 2 was launched first, on August 20, 1977, followed by Voyager 1 in September. But because Voyager 1 was following a faster, shorter trajectory, it arrived at Jupiter first, on March 5, 1979. Voyager 2 arrived on July 9, 1979.

Postcards to the Future

Because he knew that the Pioneer spacecraft would eventually leave the solar system and enter interstellar space, astronomer Carl Sagan devised a message for whomever might eventually discover these tiny probes from Earth. It was a little like putting a message in a bottle and tossing it into the ocean.

These messages took the form of small, gold-plated plaques attached to the sides of the spacecraft. Engraved on the plaques were diagrams showing our location in the Milky Way galaxy as well as a drawing of a naked man and woman depicted next to a drawing of the spacecraft.

No one expects to receive a reply in the near future. Pioneer 10 is heading toward the star Aldebaran in the constellation Taurus and will take more than two million years to get there, while Pioneer 11 will pass near one of the stars in the constellation of Aquila in about four million years. But if intelligent life exists elsewhere in the galaxy, then they might be able to decipher the plaques and learn about our existence in turn.

Sagan suggested a similar idea for the Voyager spacecraft. This time, he came up with a much more elaborate idea: a record that would contain images and sounds of our world.

Sagan formed a committee that selected 115 images of our planet as well as sounds such as wind, surf, whale and bird songs, and selections of music from different periods and cultures. His committee added recorded greetings from the people of Earth, spoken in fifty-five different languages. All of this material was recorded on a 12-inch (30 cm) disk of gold-plated copper. Engraved on its surface is a diagram showing how the record can be played.

Between the two spacecraft, fifty-two thousand images of Jupiter and its moons far exceeding in quality anything taken by earthbound telescopes were sent back to Earth.

The biggest surprise to come out of the mission to Jupiter was probably that Io, one of Jupiter's four largest moons, had active volcanoes. It proved to have the most active volcanoes—up to four hundred—in the entire solar system.

Volcanoes, Oceans, and Tides

The volcanoes of Jupiter's moon Io and the oceans of liquid water buried beneath the icy crusts of Europa, Ganymede, and Enceladus have one thing in common: tides. As a moon orbits a planet, the planet's gravity pulls on the side of the moon that is closest to it but pulls less hard on the side that is farther away. This is because the force of gravity decreases with distance. The uneven pull is called a tide. Tides can cause a moon to flex like a rubber ball being squeezed in your fist. Larger planets have stronger gravity, and so planets such as Jupiter and Saturn can have interesting tidal effects on their moons. Tidal flexing can generate great amounts of heat, enough to keep the subsurface oceans of Europa and Enceladus in liquid form and to power Io's volcanoes.

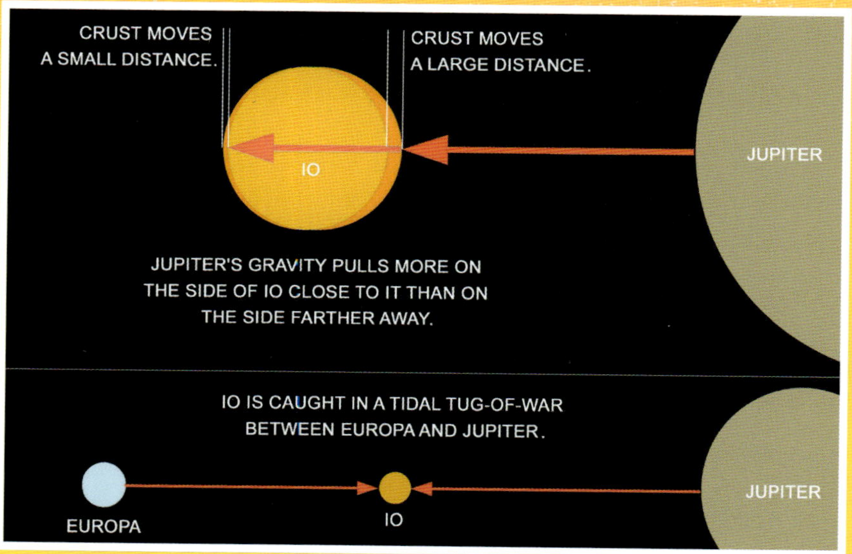

This diagram shows how the gravitational forces of Jupiter and Europa cause Io's intense volcanic activity.

The Voyager spacecraft continued on to Saturn, arriving nine months apart, in November 1980 and August 1981. Scientists learned that Saturn's atmosphere, like Jupiter's, is composed almost entirely of hydrogen and helium. Where Jupiter is covered by colorful clouds and swirling, hurricane-like storms, Saturn looks almost bland by comparison in the images Voyager spacecraft sent back to Earth. But the weather on Saturn is anything but bland. The spacecraft measured wind speeds of up to 500 miles (804 km) an hour. This is due in part to Saturn's rapid rotation: The Voyagers measured that each day on Saturn is just ten hours and thirty-nine minutes. They found that Saturn is a cold world as well. Temperatures in the upper atmosphere were a chilly −312°F (−191°C). Like Earth, Saturn has auroras flicking around its north and south poles as its powerful magnetic field attracts particles in the solar wind.

After Saturn, Voyager 1's path took it out of the solar system. Voyager 2 continued on to visit two more planets: Uranus and Neptune.

Uranus is more than twice as far from the sun as Saturn, and Neptune is three times farther, so far away that even in the largest earthbound telescopes they appeared as little more than blue-green pinheads with no detail visible. All that astronomers knew about them was that despite their smaller size, they resemble Jupiter and Saturn in being made mostly of gases and ice. Both planets have moons, with Neptune having an especially large one, Triton, which is almost half the size of Mercury. Uranus also possesses rings, like Saturn. But unlike Saturn's, Uranus's rings are very narrow and very dark, meaning they are probably made of dust rather than ice. These rings had been discovered from Earth when an astronomer noticed background stars dimming as the rings passed in front of them.

What makes Uranus unique among the planets in our solar system is its very unusual axial tilt. The planets in the solar system sit in line with the sun's equator on an imaginary plane called the ecliptic. Earth is tipped about 23.5 degrees with respect to the ecliptic plane, giving rise to the seasons: As Earth progresses through its yearly orbit, its Northern and Southern Hemispheres alternate in leaning toward the sun. The axis of Uranus, however, is tipped more than 90 degrees. This means that for nearly half its year—which lasts for eighty-four Earth years—its north pole points toward the sun, and for the other half of its orbit, its north pole is in darkness. Scientists still wonder how Uranus acquired this tilt and what effects the tilt might have on it.

Voyager 2 arrived at Uranus on November 4, 1985. It explored Uranus and its system of moons for the next three and a half months.

The spacecraft confirmed that the atmosphere of Uranus, like that of Jupiter and Saturn, is mostly hydrogen and helium. About 2 percent of the atmosphere is methane, which accounts for Uranus's greenish color since the gas absorbs red light and reflects blue and green. Voyager 2 also took measurements of the planet's magnetic field and its temperature (a frigid −353°F, or −214°C) and discovered not only two more rings but also ten more moons. The strangest of these newly discovered moons is probably Miranda, which looks as if it were assembled from spare parts. Its surface is a maze of ridges, canyons, cliffs, grooves, and craters. Scientists speculate that it got its weird appearance because it really *was* assembled from spare parts. Millions of years ago, Miranda may have suffered a devastating impact by a large asteroid that shattered the moon into hundreds of large pieces. As these orbited Uranus, they slowly drifted back together, creating Miranda's haphazard appearance.

Next on Voyager 2's itinerary was Neptune, which it flew by on August 25, 1989. Images revealed a planet that was almost a twin of Uranus. The main difference was that where Uranus was an almost featureless blue ball, Neptune had a dark, oval-shaped storm. Similar in appearance to Jupiter's famous Great Red Spot, Neptune's storm was quickly dubbed the Great Dark Spot. Voyager 2 also found six new moons, and it discovered that Neptune was circled by four narrow dark rings.

An adjustment to the spacecraft's course took it close to Neptune's large moon, Triton, which is nearly the size of Earth's moon. It found that Triton had not only a very thin atmosphere but was also geologically active, observing several large geysers spewing material high above the moon's surface. Despite being one of the coldest bodies in the solar system (Voyager 2 measured its surface temperature at −391°F [−235°C]), to produce geysers, it must have a warm interior. Scientists believe this heat is generated by tidal forces created deep inside the moon by Neptune's gravity, in the same way that Jupiter powers the volcanoes on Io.

Exploring the Giants

After learning so much about the outer planets from the Voyager missions, NASA launched two more major expeditions to Saturn and Jupiter in 1997 and 2011, respectively. Arriving at Saturn in 2004, Cassini orbited the planet for thirteen years before finally running out of fuel. On its way to the ringed planet, it delivered the Huygens lander, a project of the European Space Agency, which set down on the surface of Saturn's giant moon, Titan. Images revealed an almost Earthlike world with dunes, mountains, river valleys, and seas. Earthlike, except for its frigid temperatures and atmosphere of nitrogen and methane.

During its 294 orbits of Saturn, Cassini flew within 1,012 miles (1,628 km) of its cloud tops, made four passes through the rings, and took nearly half a million close-up photos of the planet and several of its satellites. Images of Enceladus surprised scientists when they revealed the little moon erupting vast plumes of water ice into space. Cassini even catalogued six new moons in Saturn's collection.

Where Are the Voyagers Today?

The Voyagers were meant to last only five years, but like many other NASA spacecraft they have far exceeded expectations. More than forty-five years later, both spacecraft are far beyond the planets and are deep into interstellar space. Voyager 1 is almost 15 billion miles (24 billion km) from Earth, about 161 times the distance of Earth from the sun. A signal traveling at the speed of light takes more than twenty-two hours to reach Earth from that distance. Voyager 2, meanwhile, is more than 12.3 billion miles (19.9 billion km) from Earth. Both spacecraft continue to radio information back to Earth. In July 2023, communication with the Voyager 2 spacecraft was temporarily lost while its antenna was not pointed directly at Earth, but contact was reestablished in October of that year.

Both spacecraft—now dubbed the Voyager Interstellar Mission—have returned valuable information about the outer edge of the heliosphere, a region 120 times farther away from the sun than Earth. This is where the solar wind meets the cold interstellar medium. The boundary between the two is called the heliopause, and it forms something like a vast bubble surrounding the solar system.

The last photograph Cassini took shows the region where it soon plunged into Saturn's atmosphere.

NASA's Juno orbiter arrived at Jupiter on July 4, 2014, five years after leaving Earth. It went into a polar orbit around the planet, circling Jupiter from pole to pole while Jupiter rotated beneath it, allowing it to eventually pass over every part of the planet. Near the end of the prime mission, as the spacecraft's orbit evolved, flybys of the moon Ganymede initiated Juno's transition into a full Jupiter system explorer. Juno will continue exploring Jupiter and its moons through September 2025, or until the spacecraft runs out of power and fuel.

Why is studying Jupiter so important? Aside from being the largest planet in the solar system—after the sun, it has the largest gravitational effect on the other planets—it gives astronomers valuable clues as to how the solar system, including Earth, was formed. Jupiter may have been the first of all the planets to form from the cloud of dust and gas that surrounded the newborn sun more than four billion years ago. It is made mostly of the same elements as the sun: hydrogen and helium. Studying Jupiter is like being able to see billions of years into the past.

Juno made an important discovery in October 2023. While scanning Jupiter's moon, Ganymede, the largest moon in the solar system (it is larger than the planet Mercury), Juno found mineral salts and organic compounds on the surface. These gave scientists clues about the deep ocean of liquid water that lies beneath the moon's icy crust. Like Earth's oceans, Ganymede's may be salty and filled with organic molecules. Kept warm by tidal heating caused by Jupiter, Ganymede's ocean could even be an abode for life.

NASA has invited the public to take part in the Juno program by making the raw, unprocessed images from Juno freely available. Most

Juno captured stunning images of Jupiter's Great Red Spot, a storm that has been raging on its surface for hundreds of years. Scientists still do not know the origin of its stark color.

images sent back to Earth by NASA spacecraft are processed before being released to the public. This is done to make sure that colors are correct and transmission flaws are removed. But with the Juno images, NASA has invited anyone interested to take the raw, unprocessed images and experiment with them, providing an opportunity to gain experience working with astronomical data.

The Frontiers of the Solar System

In October 1991, the United States Postal Service released a set of ten commemorative stamps: one for each planet, plus Earth's moon. Each stamp had a picture of a planet along with a spacecraft associated with it: Mars and the Viking Orbiter, for example, and Jupiter and Pioneer 11. The stamp for dwarf planet Pluto, though, had no spacecraft. Instead, it was labeled NOT YET EXPLORED. Many scientists took that as a challenge and began campaigning for a dedicated mission to Pluto.

With planetary scientist Alan Stern in charge as the principal investigator, NASA announced the New Horizons mission to Pluto on November 29, 2001, and five years later, the spacecraft was on its way.

Pluto is more than 3 billion miles (4.8 billion km) from Earth. To travel such an enormous distance in a reasonable amount of time, New Horizons was launched at a very high speed. Leaving Earth at 36,400 miles (58,580 km) an hour, it was the fastest object ever launched from our planet. A mere nine hours after leaving Cape Canaveral, it passed the moon—a trip nearly ten times faster than the one that the Apollo astronauts took. Even going that fast, the spacecraft took fourteen years to reach Pluto.

On its way to Pluto, New Horizons made a close flyby of Jupiter and its system of moons, taking photos and gathering data. It sent detailed images of Jupiter's rings back to Earth as well as images of one of Io's largest volcanoes erupting.

New Horizons began its encounter with Pluto on January 15, 2015, while it was still 200 million miles (322 million km) from the dwarf planet. It made its closest approach on July 14 of that year, passing within 7,800

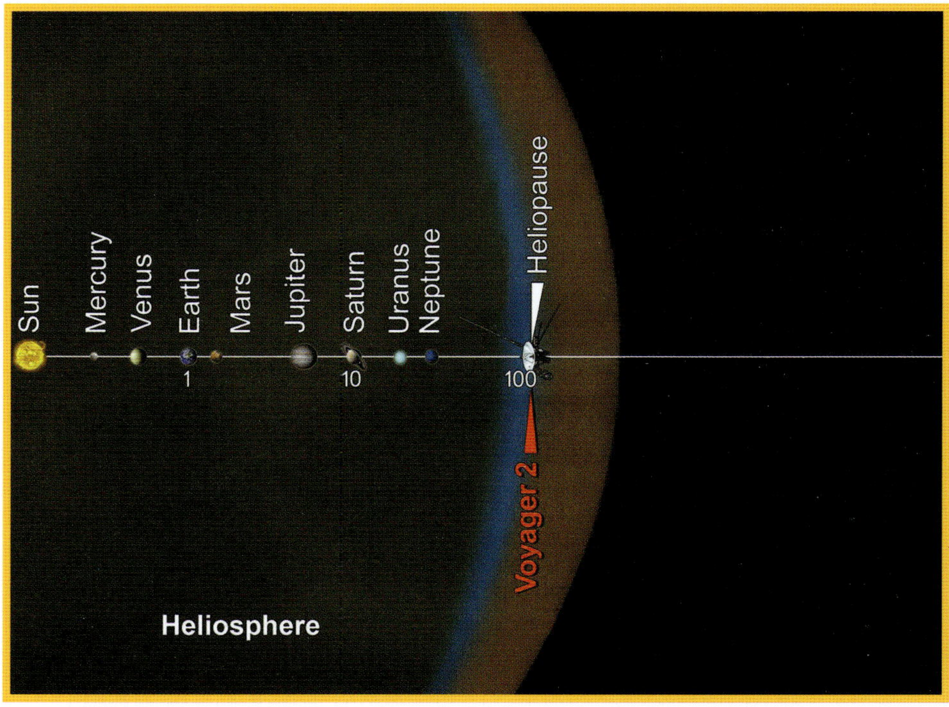

Following Voyager 1's passage in 2012, Voyager 2 passed into interstellar space, out beyond the reaches of the sun's influence (the heliosphere), in 2018. Scientists are unsure how much longer the spacecraft will transmit data to Earth.

miles (12,553 km) of Pluto. In all, it gathered nearly six thousand images of Pluto and its five moons as well as valuable information from 256 separate observations using seven scientific instruments, including one developed by students at the University of Colorado that measured the amount of dust found in the outer solar system. In addition to cameras, New Horizons had other instruments, including three that measured the composition and structure of Pluto's atmosphere and one that studied the solar wind. Transmitting all the data it collected to Earth took fifteen months.

Stern and his team discovered that despite being one of the coldest places in the solar system, Pluto showed signs of activity and evidence of recent eruptions of ice volcanoes. The lack of craters on Pluto's surface surprised scientists because it suggests that the surface of Pluto is relatively young, meaning that it is constantly being replaced by glaciers and icy material flowing from volcanoes and geysers. The most distinguishing visual feature on Pluto, the pink, heart-shaped plain called Sputnik Planitia, is the largest glacier in the solar system. The scientists found that Pluto has large mountains made entirely of ice up to 15,000 feet (4,572 m) high. Pluto even has an atmosphere—a very thin one but dense enough for clouds. If you stood on its surface and looked up, its sky would be blue.

On Beyond Pluto

Extending past Pluto is a vast region filled with icy bodies, some of them as large as or even slightly larger than Pluto. This region is called the Kuiper Belt after Gerard Kuiper, an astronomer who, in 1951, was the first to suggest that the solar system might be surrounded by a vast belt of icy bodies extending from between thirty and fifty-five times farther from the sun than Earth—roughly the same distance of Pluto's orbit. Nearly forty years later, astronomers David Jewitt and Jane Luu made the first direct observations of a Kuiper Belt object, which was later named Albion. While many Kuiper Belt objects have since been detected and measured, and Pluto has since been recognized as a Kuiper Belt object itself, they are all much too small and too far away for even the most powerful telescopes on Earth to image. New Horizons presented the perfect opportunity to get more information about the Kuiper Belt.

New Horizons provided detailed photographs of Pluto's surface, allowing scientists to create the first true-color images of the distant planet.

Nine years later and after traveling a billion miles (1.6 billion km) past Pluto, New Horizons flew by its second target, a Kuiper Belt object called Arrokoth, and sent back the first pictures of one of these mysterious bodies. Arrokoth turned out to be very strange. It looked like two different objects, one almost spherical and the other shaped like a pancake, had stuck together. It is about 22 miles (35 km) long, 12 miles (19 km) wide, and 6 miles (10 km) thick. It probably got its strange shape when two Kuiper Belt objects collided and stuck together, creating a contact binary. Some scientists hypothesize that Arrokoth is a relic from the formation of our solar system 4.5 billion years ago, when small objects were colliding and sticking together to make larger ones—in the same process that eventually produced the planets.

Exploring Asteroids

Asteroids are bodies made of rock and metal. Most asteroids orbit the sun in the asteroid belt between Mars and Jupiter, but some are drifting through the solar system on other trajectories. Asteroids can be a threat to life on Earth, as the impact of even a small one would have devastating consequences.

One of NASA's recent projects has been the detection of potentially dangerous asteroids. Its first goal was to achieve a kind of early warning system: the ability to detect an asteroid long before it posed a hazard to our planet. To help with establishing an early warning system, NASA launched the Near-Earth Object Wide Field Infrared Survey Explorer satellite into Earth's orbit in 2009 to perform an accurate survey of comets and objects close to Earth that might pose a threat to our planet.

NASA's second goal was to devise some way to do something about the hazardous objects, which proved to be a difficult problem. Destroying an asteroid that was large enough to be a threat would be like trying to blow up a mountain. And even if an asteroid were destroyed—perhaps by using thermonuclear devices (atomic bombs)—much of the debris would remain on its trajectory toward Earth. So instead of one impact, there would be hundreds scattered across the globe.

A better idea is to try to move the asteroid. If this were done early enough, it would not take much of a nudge to alter the asteroid's path so that by the time it intersects Earth's orbit, it would miss us.

To test this idea, NASA launched the Double Asteroid Redirection Test in November 2021 to the asteroid Didymos. Didymos, which is about 2,560 feet (780 m) wide, had a small moon of its own, Dimorphos, just 530 feet (160 m) across. Astronomers knew the orbit of Dimorphos very precisely. The goal was to impact the spacecraft directly into Dimorphos to see if the collision would change its orbit. Ten months after it was launched on November 24, 2022, the 1,260 pound (572 kg) spacecraft slammed into the little moon at 14,000 miles (22,530 km) per hour.

The experiment was a success. Before the impact, Dimorphos orbited Didymos once every eleven hours and fifty-five minutes. The impact shortened this time to eleven hours and twenty-three minutes—a difference of thirty-two minutes. This would be more than enough deviation to deflect the path of an asteroid headed toward Earth—as long as we acted in time.

Ceres

NASA launched its Dawn spacecraft in 2007 to explore the second-largest body in the asteroid belt, Vesta. It arrived in 2011 and orbited Vesta for over a year, taking photos and gathering data. In September 2012, Dawn left Vesta to travel to the dwarf planet Ceres. Orbiting in the main asteroid belt between Mars and Jupiter, Ceres is the largest of all the asteroids. It was the first asteroid ever discovered—in 1801—and is large enough, at almost 600 miles (965 km) in diameter, to be spherical. Gravity is responsible for shaping moons and planets into spheres. If a body is large enough, the pull of its gravity will be stronger than the material it is made of. Since gravity pulls equally in all directions, this will cause the object to take the shape of a sphere—which is why planets are spherical, yet many smaller asteroids are more irregular in shape.

Dawn's observations of Ceres showed scientists that the asteroid was composed of a rocky core covered in water ice. Dawn found that about 25 percent of Ceres might be ice. It even has a very thin atmosphere containing water vapor. Since it is one of the few large bodies in the solar system that has water, scientists think that Ceres could possibly contain fossilized microbes. It is unlikely that anything might be living on Ceres today. Aside from being very cold (−100°F, or −73°C, during the day and −225°F, or −143°C, at night), scientists believe Ceres has no magnetic field to shield its surface from deadly solar radiation.

Bennu

The small asteroid Bennu was originally called 1999 RQ36. But it was renamed after nine-year-old student Michael Puzio from North Carolina suggested Bennu, the name of an ancient Egyptian deity. Bennu was NASA's target for its first attempt to retrieve a sample from an asteroid and return it to Earth. The mission, Origins, Spectral Interpretation, Resource Identification, and Security—Regolith Explorer (OSIRIS-REx) was launched in 2016. After arriving at Bennu, the spacecraft gathered samples of dust and pebbles from the surface of the asteroid. As the spacecraft swung back past Earth on September 24, 2023, it dropped the capsule containing the samples, which descended by parachute to scientists in Utah. The first tests of the samples revealed that they were rich in carbon, water, and iron-based minerals.

Meanwhile, OSIRIS-REx, under a new name, Origins, Spectral Interpretation, Resource Identification, and Security—Apophis Explorer

(OSIRIS-APEX), continued on for a new mission: to rendezvous with the over 1,000-foot-wide (305 m) asteroid Apophis. The spacecraft will reach Apophis in 2029, when the asteroid will approach within 20,000 miles (32,187 km) of Earth: less than one-tenth the distance separating Earth and the moon. OSIRIS-APEX will go into orbit around Apophis soon after it passes Earth to see how the close encounter with our planet might have affected the asteroid's orbit, rotation, and surface.

The Trojans

Launched on October 16, 2021, NASA's Lucy spacecraft will explore eleven different asteroids. On November 1, 2023, it flew by its first target and shocked scientists with what it discovered: The asteroid Dinkinesh had a small moon of its own. Dinkinesh is a main belt asteroid, meaning that it lies in the region of asteroids orbiting between Mars and Jupiter, and is about half a mile (0.8 km) wide. Its moon is less than 800 feet (243 m) wide and has a strange shape. Scientists realized the moon was a contact binary, much like the Kuiper Belt's Arrokoth. After studying Dinkinesh and two other main belt asteroids, Lucy will move on to its ultimate goal: a group of asteroids called the Trojans.

There are two special places around Jupiter, 60 degrees ahead of the planet in its orbit and 60 degrees behind it, where its gravity combines with that of the sun to form stable regions. These are called Lagrange points after Italian French mathematician Joseph-Louis Lagrange, who first suggested their existence in 1772. Objects in these areas will remain there, moving along in the same orbit but never getting any nearer to Jupiter, nor any farther away. Over millions of years, a number of small asteroids have drifted into these points and were trapped there. These asteroids are called Trojans.

Every planet has a pair of Lagrange points along its orbit, including Earth. NASA has taken advantage of the stability produced by the gravitational forces at Earth's own Lagrange points and placed spacecraft in orbit there, including the James Webb Space Telescope. Orbiting at a Lagrange point means that the telescope is always well away from any interference from Earth and the moon, yet always stays the same distance from Earth.

Psyche

Asteroids are made either mostly of rock or mostly of metal (while a few are half rock and half metal). A metallic asteroid might consist of as much as 80 percent iron with the remaining 20 percent nickel and other metals. The asteroid Psyche is a small, potato-shaped body only 173 miles (278 km) across at its widest point and 144 miles (232 km) long. It appears to be made of as much as 60 percent iron and nickel. Because the cores of such planets as Earth and Mercury are largely made of iron and nickel, scientists believe Psyche may be the core of a much larger body that was shattered by an impact millions of years ago. The cores of most planets and large asteroids are buried under hundreds or even thousands of miles of outer crust, but Psyche doesn't have a thick crust. NASA's Psyche mission, launched in October 2023 and arriving at the asteroid in 2029, will be a unique opportunity to explore the core of a planet, even if it had been a very small one. Studying Psyche may provide valuable information about how the core of our own planet came to be.

Trailing Comets

NASA has flown eight missions to explore comets, though not all have been successful. Among those that achieved their goals is Stardust. In 2004 it collected samples from the coma—the cloud of dust and gas that surrounded the nucleus—of comet 81P/Wild 2. It returned these samples to Earth in a special capsule. After completing this part of its mission, Stardust was renamed Stardust-NExT and sent to comet Tempel 1, which it flew past on February 14, 2011.

Another successful comet mission was Deep Impact. During its nine-year mission, Deep Impact's goal was to probe beneath the surface of a comet. To do this, it launched an impactor weighing 820 pounds (372 kg) at the comet. It then analyzed the cloud of materials from deep beneath the surface of the comet that launched into space as a result of the collision. The impactor also carried a camera that took close-up images of the comet's surface and sent them to the main spacecraft seconds before it hit. Among the surprising results was how porous the comet nucleus was. It was almost 75 percent empty space.

The collision between Tempel 1 and the impactor created as much energy as 5 tons (4.5 t) of dynamite and made the comet shine six times brighter than normal.

While Kuiper Belt objects, asteroids, and comets are intrinsically interesting for astronomers, they also help us to better understand our own planet. Many of these bodies are leftovers from the formation of our solar system. They are like windows into the distant past, helping us to better understand how all the planets formed, including Earth. And the better we understand where our planet came from, the better we can understand how it works.

Chapter 9

Keeping an Eye on Earth

NASA is famous for its missions to study and explore outer space, from the moon, sun, and planets to other stars and galaxies, but it also closely watches our own world. It oversees the collection of hundreds of thousands of measurements taken every day, all over the world. Weather satellites report on sea and air temperatures, wind speed, rainfall, snow, and cloud cover. The information from these satellites has been invaluable for farmers who need to know the best time for planting crops, shipping companies that need to navigate around icebergs, cities along the coast that might need to evacuate in advance of a dangerous hurricane, and even hikers looking for a perfect hiking trail. Scientists also use the information for tracking the effects of global climate change.

By mapping the snow cover in mountains, NASA satellites can help predict floods and the amount of water available for power generation. Monitoring the movement of glaciers and the amount of ice in the Arctic and Antarctic regions over decades has helped scientists predict how ocean levels might rise over the next century. NASA can also detect, track, and study the effects of oil spills and industrial waste in oceans, wildfires, and air pollution from industry.

Satellites even study the weather in outer space. One such satellite is the Deep Space Climate Observatory, which monitors activity on the sun, looking for events such as solar flares that cause disruptions in

Satellite images of hurricanes help meteorologists predict how devastating the storms might be. With climate change causing more severe storms more frequently, satellite data will be even more important.

communication and navigation, power blackouts, and radiation hazards.

In 1970 Congress created the National Oceanographic and Atmospheric Administration (NOAA) to study Earth's climate and weather, and it has worked with NASA ever since. The space agency takes care of launching weather satellites, and NOAA administers them and processes the data they send back. Hundreds of satellites have been launched whose sole purpose is to study Earth, to understand how it works, and to see how it is changing. NASA's research and discoveries are becoming even more important as the global climate crisis escalates. These projects provide researchers with the necessary data to address key questions about global climate change.

All of these things go toward making our planet a cleaner, safer place to live.

While weather balloons provide essential information, they are also a hazard to Earth's ecosystems. When they reach a certain altitude, they burst, and the latex they are made of falls to Earth, where it can harm wildlife.

From Balloons to Satellites

Until the 1960s, weather balloons had been the main source of information about the upper atmosphere. They carried instruments that measured temperature, humidity, and other qualities and sent the information by radio to waiting scientists on the ground. But most weather balloons were launched from land, since launching and then tracking a balloon over oceans wasn't easy, and in any case, it was hard to predict where a balloon would go.

In 1959 scientist Lewis Kaplan came up with the idea for the modern weather satellite. He suggested that Earth satellites using instruments called sounders would be able to take measurements vertically, through every layer of the atmosphere, revealing temperature, amounts of water vapor, and other details that would allow for accurate weather predictions.

The first weather satellite, the Television Infrared Observation Satellite (TIROS-1), was launched into orbit on April 1, 1960. It carried two television cameras and two tape recorders. For seventy-eight days, it sent back more than twenty thousand photos of Earth as seen from space. The satellite ceased operations before it could help to predict a deadly hurricane that occurred that spring, but the data it provided scientists encouraged President Kennedy to add $75 million to NASA's budget to "help give us at the earliest possible time a satellite system for worldwide weather observation."

This weather satellite was soon followed by seven satellites called

Nimbus, launched between 1964 and 1978. *Nimbus* means "cloud" in Latin. Carrying twenty-four instruments each, the Nimbus satellites gathered much more information about Earth's weather than TIROS-1. The satellites were also in polar orbits, much like the orbit of Juno around Jupiter.

In addition to satellites in polar orbits, weather scientists use geostationary satellites. These orbit at just the right distance from Earth so that the movement of the satellite matches Earth's rotation, and the satellite appears to remain over the same spot on Earth all the time. The measurements taken by such satellites enable scientists to see weather patterns in motion.

Nimbus 3, launched in 1969, was the first to follow Kaplan's original idea of sounding the atmosphere. It measured levels of temperature, moisture, and water vapor from the upper atmosphere down to the surface of Earth. Through Nimbus 3, NASA was able to obtain data from regions otherwise inaccessible: above the oceans or over the polar regions. "It was like putting a thermometer at all different levels of the atmosphere and all over the globe," said Chris Barnet, an adviser for NASA.

The first sounding satellites measured infrared radiation. Everything that is warmer than freezing radiates infrared. Clouds radiate, the ground radiates—even trees and human beings radiate. By measuring the amount of radiation emitted by different kinds of molecules—such as oxygen, carbon dioxide, or water—scientists can measure temperature and moisture at different altitudes. But infrared has one big problem: If clouds are dense enough, they will block infrared radiation. And clouds cover half of Earth at any one time. To resolve this, engineers added microwave sensors to newer satellites. Microwaves can penetrate clouds, allowing scientists to obtain data right down to the surface of Earth.

The Earth Observing System

NASA's Earth Observing System (EOS) is a collection of twenty-six satellites that closely observe conditions on the surface of our planet, as well as its biosphere (the region of Earth's surface that contains life), atmosphere, weather, and oceans. The satellites even monitor the effects of volcanic eruptions. The first of the system's satellites was launched in 1999.

One of the main drivers behind the EOS program is the changing climate of our planet. According to NASA, the goal of EOS is to "provide in-depth scientific understanding about the functioning of Earth as a system. It is envisioned that such scientific knowledge will provide the foundation for understanding the natural and human-induced variations in Earth's climate system and also provide a sound basis for environmental policy decision making." In addition to the scientific information the satellites provide, "it was also envisioned that EOS would have practical societal benefits in the form of providing scientific knowledge toward the efficient production of food and fiber, management of fresh water resources, and improvement of air quality."

Chapter 10

Observing the Universe

NASA has long been interested in what caused the beginning of the solar system and how life began on our planet. Studying our solar system helps to answer some of these questions. The sun, though, is just one star among billions in the universe. How was it formed? How did its collection of planets come to be? To find out, NASA has had to look far beyond our own local neighborhood. A series of powerful telescopes, some carried far above Earth by aircraft and others orbiting in space, have studied other stars and galaxies, providing clues to the origin of Earth and life. These telescopes have observed stars, solar systems, and even planets in every stage of formation. They have even found planets circling distant stars that may be very similar to our own world.

Astronomy from the Sky

Observing the universe from an airplane instead of from a ground-based observatory has a lot of advantages. The atmosphere of our planet is often filled with clouds, preventing a clear view of the sky. The atmosphere close to the ground is also always moving, acting like a kind of lens or a wobbly piece of glass that distorts stars and planets viewed from the ground. Another problem is that the water vapor in Earth's atmosphere filters out certain wavelengths of light, such as infrared, which prevents astronomers from being able to study the entire spectrum of an object. This is why observatories are so often built on the tops of mountains: to get them high above as much of the atmosphere as possible.

An airplane can get even higher, and because it's mobile, it can study phenomena occurring in regions that lack an observatory. For instance, when a solar eclipse occurs, and the moon passes in front of the sun, casting a shadow on Earth's surface, the path of the moon's shadow can fall almost anywhere on Earth. If the path doesn't fall over an observatory, the astronomers who work there are out of luck. Astronomers aboard a telescope-carrying aircraft, however, can travel to the shadow. And because the shadow of the moon passes over the surface of Earth as Earth rotates, the maximum length of time anyone on the ground can witness an eclipse—from the moment the moon starts to pass over the sun to when the sun reappears—is about seven minutes. An aircraft can follow the path of the eclipse, staying within the shadow of the moon for much longer.

Space telescopes overcome the problem of atmospheric interference, but repairing or upgrading a space telescope is difficult, expensive, and sometimes impossible to do. An airborne observatory can easily undergo repairs or improvements any time the aircraft returns to its base.

NASA began conducting airborne astronomy in 1965. It modified a jet airliner to carry a telescope and other instruments, giving astronomers the opportunity to follow the totality of a solar eclipse. Three years later, NASA modified a Learjet—a small business jet—to carry 12-inch (30.5 cm) telescopes to study Venus in infrared light.

These projects proved to be so successful that NASA created the Kuiper Airborne Observatory in 1975. The observatory was a large cargo airplane fitted with a 36-inch (91 cm) reflecting telescope. Inside the aircraft was a complete laboratory for the astronomers. The observatory operated for twenty years, producing a large body of valuable information about the solar system and the universe. Among its discoveries was Pluto's atmosphere and Uranus's dark, narrow rings. It discovered water in comets as well as Jupiter's atmosphere and the existence of complex organic molecules in interstellar space. Flying above Earth's shield of water vapor, observatory astronomers were even able to take the temperature of a returning space shuttle's heat shield by measuring its infrared radiation.

The observatory was replaced in 2010 by the Stratospheric Observatory for Infrared Astronomy, a collaboration with Germany's space agency. This time, a much larger aircraft was converted, a retired Boeing 747 passenger jet, which NASA equipped with a 106-inch (2.7 m) telescope provided by the German agency. The aircraft allowed the twenty scientists and technicians aboard to conduct observations from as high as 45,000 feet (13.7 km).

This observatory was responsible for a long list of discoveries. Among them were the observation of the birth of stars and new solar systems and the discovery of black holes at the center of distant galaxies.

Observatories in Space

As effective, simple, and economical as airborne observatories may be, and despite the higher costs and risks of sending things into orbit, there are immense advantages to having telescopes in space. Keenly aware of the limitations to their observations caused by the atmosphere, astronomers had dreamed of studying space directly from space since the 1920s.

NASA's Astrophysics Division is specifically devoted to studying the universe and how it works. Its scientists look for planets beyond our solar system where life may have evolved; explore how black holes affect space, time, and matter; and look for evidence of the mysterious, invisible dark energy and dark matter that seem to make up the bulk of our universe.

In addition to the Stratospheric Observatory for Infrared Astronomy, among the many instruments used by scientists in the Astrophysics Division are several space telescopes, orbiting far removed from the interference of Earth's atmosphere and vibrations.

The Great Observatories

NASA's Great Observatories program launched four telescopes into space between 1990 and 2003. Each was designed to explore a different part of the electromagnetic spectrum. The first, the Hubble Space Telescope, observed the universe in the visible spectrum—the same range as the human eye.

Inside the Pillars of Creation nebula, stars are forming. The Webb image (*left*) is in the infrared spectrum. Scientists can learn more about structures in space by comparing images taken by Webb and those taken by Hubble (*right*).

Named for astronomer Edwin Hubble, the Hubble Space Telescope has been operating continuously since 1990. It has made more than 1.5 million observations of planets, stars, and galaxies. Every week it transmits 140 gigabytes of data back to Earth. That's equal to about thirty thousand MP3 files.

The telescope is the size of a school bus and has a mirror 7.9 feet (2.4 m) in diameter. The size of a mirror in a telescope is important: The larger the mirror is, the more light it can collect, and the more light it collects, the more detail it can resolve. The pupil of a human eye is about 0.15 inches (4 mm) in diameter. The opening, or aperture, of the Hubble telescope is 94 inches (2.4 m). With such a large "pupil," Hubble's mirror collects sixty thousand times the amount of light the human eye does. This means it can detect objects sixty thousand times dimmer than the human eye can perceive.

Five instruments are attached to the telescope. Three cameras record images in visible light as well as near-ultraviolet and near-infrared—wavelengths just slightly beyond those the human eye can detect. Two spectrographs analyze the light from stars and galaxies, giving scientists clues about their chemical composition. The telescope also has fine guidance sensors to help it point at its targets.

Since Hubble began operating, it has made countless discoveries. Among these is the age of the universe (about fourteen billion years old), several black holes, and even the composition of the atmospheres of distant exoplanets.

Named after gamma-ray physicist Arthur Compton, the next space telescope in the program was the Compton Gamma Ray Observatory, which was launched by astronauts aboard the space shuttle Atlantis in 1991. Instead of visible light, it specialized in studying light with very small wavelengths, including the X-rays and gamma rays emitted by the sun and other stars. It operated until 2000, when an equipment failure led NASA to deorbit the telescope and allow it to burn up in Earth's atmosphere.

The Chandra X-ray Observatory, named after physicist Subrahmanyan Chandrasekhar, was launched from the space shuttle Columbia in 1999. X-rays are created when matter is heated to millions of degrees. Temperatures like these are produced by powerful magnetic fields, extreme gravity, or events such as an exploding star. The ability to detect X-rays enables scientists to locate objects giving off tremendous heat or gravitational forces, such as black holes.

The last of the Great Observatory telescopes, the Spitzer Space Telescope, was launched in 2003 and retired in 2020. It was designed to observe the infrared universe. Infrared radiation—which humans cannot see but instead can feel as heat—is better than visible light at penetrating through clouds of dust. This means Spitzer could see details hidden from Hubble, such as stars embedded in clouds of dark dust or gas.

The James Webb Space Telescope

Named for James Webb, the director of NASA from 1961 to 1968, the James Webb Space Telescope is a joint project of NASA, the Canadian Space Agency, and the European Space Agency. An infrared instrument designed to complement Hubble, it is also a more sensitive telescope, able to resolve finer details due to its larger mirror.

The Webb telescope shields its instruments from light and heat with layers of protective material. Its instruments won't work if they are too warm or a bright source of light shines on them.

The larger a mirror is the more difficult it is to make. To obtain the detailed information scientists wanted, the mirror needed to be 21 feet 4 inches (6.5 m) wide—nearly three times wider than Hubble's mirror and with more than seven times the surface area. In addition to the difficulty in manufacturing such a large mirror, it would be extremely heavy if it were made of glass like the mirror in the Hubble Space Telescope.

To solve this problem, engineers decided to make the mirror of beryllium, a lightweight metal that can be polished to a mirrorlike smoothness, and instead of one large mirror, the new mirror was made of eighteen hexagonal segments that could fold up. This enabled scientists to use a smaller launch vehicle. Another advantage of a mirror like this is that each segment can be adjusted individually, allowing scientists to fine-tune the focus with great accuracy.

Among the goals for the Webb telescope are to investigate the origins of the universe and the formation of the first galaxies, to study the birth of stars and planetary systems, and to search for signs of life in those systems.

The telescope was launched on December 25, 2021, from Kourou, French Guiana, on a European Space Agency Ariane 5 rocket. French

Guiana, which is on the north coast of South America, is an ideal location for a spaceport. Since it is so close to the equator, the spin of Earth adds an additional 1,038 miles (1,670 km) per hour to the rocket. The telescope unfolded once it reached its position in Earth's orbit, and then went live and began returning images on July 12, 2022.

The telescope has already made several significant discoveries. It took the first direct image of an exoplanet, a giant world eight times the size of Jupiter, orbiting a star called HIP 65426. It recorded the spectrum of the atmosphere of another exoplanet, WASP-39 b, and found that it is composed of water vapor, sulfur dioxide, carbon monoxide, sodium, and potassium—the most detailed analysis ever made of the atmosphere of an exoplanet. Sulphur dioxide is created by the action of sunlight in a process called photochemistry, and this was the first time the process had been observed taking place on another planet.

Roman Space Telescope

The Roman Space Telescope, scheduled for launch in 2027, was named for Nancy Grace Roman, the first woman executive at NASA and its first chief astronomer. The mirror in the telescope will be the same size as Hubble's but will cover one hundred times the area, capturing more of the sky in a single image. During its five-year mission, Roman will examine the light from more than a billion galaxies and is expected to locate more than twenty-six hundred new exoplanets, an estimate based on the number of exoplanets already found.

The Planet Hunter

The Transiting Exoplanet Survey Satellite is a space telescope designed to search for exoplanets using the transit method, a technique for finding exoplanets that looks for the slight dimming of a star when one or more of its planets pass between the star and the observatory. The amount of dimming and its duration can inform scientists about the size and orbit of the planet. Since its launch in 2018, this telescope has found sixty-six new exoplanets with twenty-one hundred more potential detections.

In 2019 it discovered its first Earth-sized planet. The planet, HD 21749 c, is about 89 percent of Earth's diameter. It orbits a red dwarf about 70 percent as massive as our sun. The rocky planet orbits very close to its star, circling it in less than eight days. Since its surface temperature is probably about 800°F (427°C), HD 21749 c may be Earth-sized, but it would not be very Earthlike.

This telescope recently discovered another Earth-sized planet, LP 791-18 d, that may be covered in active volcanoes. These are caused by a gravitational tug-of-war between the planet's star and an outer planet, LP 791-18 c, giving rise to tidal forces that cause the interior of the planet to heat up.

Despite the possibility of intense volcanic activity, LP 791-18 d is a candidate for the search for life. The planet sits near the star's Goldilocks zone, the region around a star where the temperature is just right for liquid water to exist on the surface of an orbiting planet. Scientists believe the exoplanet's volcanoes may have even created an atmosphere.

Chapter 11

The First *A* in NASA

It's sometimes easy to forget what the first *A* in NASA stands for. NASA itself has never forgotten that it means "aeronautics," and the agency has continually contributed to developments in aviation technology and safety even after its evolution from NACA to NASA. "At NASA," said NASA Administrator Bill Nelson in June 2023, "our eyes are not just focused on stars but also fixated on the sky."

Unusual Flying Objects

NASA has never been afraid to experiment on the very fringes of what might be possible. The results of its courage include some of the most advanced and strangest aircraft to ever take to the skies. The lifting bodies that aided in the development of the Mercury, Gemini, and Apollo capsules and the design of the space shuttles are all examples of such aircraft, which would never have existed if not for NASA's philosophy of innovation.

After NACA became NASA in 1958, most of the focus of the new agency was on space travel, but they continued to make innovations in aircraft design. The engineers at Langley worked out designs for multi-mission aircraft—aircraft that would be as efficient flying at low speeds as they were at supersonic speeds—and developed the variable-sweep, or swing, wing. As the plane took off and flew at low speeds, its wings were held out straight from the fuselage. But as the plane approached the speed of sound, the wings would gradually sweep back farther and farther. Two aircraft that have used the variable-sweep wing are NASA's X-5 and the F-14 Tomcat fighter jet, but the mechanisms required to change the angle of the wings are large and heavy, so few aircraft have incorporated this design.

A strange-looking variation on the variable-sweep idea is the oblique wing. The aircraft built in the late 1970s to test this idea, the AD-1, had a long slender fuselage. The wing was mounted on a pivot on the top of the fuselage. At slow speeds, such as during takeoff, the wing would be perpendicular to the fuselage like a conventional wing to provide maximum lift and control. As the aircraft gained speed, the angle of the wing with respect to the body of the plane would increase, reducing drag and decreasing fuel consumption. Tests on the AD-1 revealed that it had very poor handling characteristics: It was difficult to fly. In 2005, with the advent of NASA's digital flight control systems, the agency began to reconsider the concept for long-range supersonic military and commercial aircraft.

NASA also continued experimenting with lifting bodies. Hyper III was a full-scale model of a lifting body developed in the late 1960s. Evolved from the M2 program, the Hyper III looked like a clothes iron with its flat bottom and sides. It had small, straight wings with no control surfaces (the flaps you see on the edges of airplane wings). On December 12, 1969, the Hyper III made its only flight when it was launched from a helicopter at 10,000 feet (3,048 m). It glided under remote control for 3 miles (5 km), turned around, and landed. Although the test was generally successful, the program was canceled after the three-minute flight because the aircraft didn't perform as efficiently as expected.

Another unusual aircraft was the tailless X-36, a small (18-foot-long, or 5.5 m), jet-propelled scale model of a theoretical advanced fighter aircraft developed in collaboration with the private aeronautics company Boeing. Since the tailless design was unstable, it was controlled by the fly-by-wire system NASA had developed (see page 115). The X-36's first flight was on May 17, 1997. It completed thirty-one successful test flights in November 1997.

NASA collaborated again with Boeing and with the US Air Force Research Laboratory to study the blended wing concept. A cross between a tailless flying wing and a conventional aircraft, the X-48B is reminiscent of several early space shuttle concepts that had taken advantage of lifting body research. A large remote-controlled model was successfully tested over eighty flights, completing the last one in 2010. Although originally funded as a study for future military aircraft, the X-48B had many characteristics—such as fuel efficiency, low noise, and a large payload in comparison to the size of the aircraft—that would make it attractive as a passenger airliner.

Next-Generation Propulsion

In addition to designing and testing unusual aircraft shapes, NASA engineers have always been interested in developing new methods of propelling aircraft, from propellers to jets to rockets.

In the late 1950s and early 1960s, NASA researched new types of propulsion that might be used to launch winged spacecraft. One result was the Liquid Air Cycle Engine, which allowed an aircraft to collect air from the atmosphere and compress it to make liquid oxygen. The oxygen was then pumped into the engines to burn the liquid hydrogen from the aircraft's fuel tanks. While the process involved some complicated technology, it would be environmentally safe as the only emission from burning hydrogen is water. This engine was briefly tested under laboratory conditions in 1960. NASA, however, lost interest in winged spacecraft, and this engine was eventually abandoned.

At the same time that its engineers were developing this engine, NASA experimented with ramjets, a technology that dates back to World War II. A ramjet is essentially a pipe that is open at both ends. As the pipe moves, air enters one end and is compressed as fuel is added. The air and fuel mixture is ignited, and the gases rushing out the other end of the pipe propel it forward. The propulsion can be powerful enough to launch a spacecraft up to speeds sufficient to enter Earth's orbit. And because the spacecraft doesn't need to carry any oxidizer to burn its fuel—it gets that from the atmosphere—it would be lighter and less expensive to launch than rocket-powered spacecraft like the space shuttles.

One of the biggest advantages of the ramjet is that it has no moving parts, so malfunctions are less common and it is simpler to maintain or repair. A ramjet spacecraft could also take off and land from conventional runways. It would not need a special launch facility like the space shuttle. The only problem with the ramjet is that it has to be already moving very fast for it to start working. Through their experiments, NASA created scramjets, a type of ramjet with combustion chambers that could function above the speed of sound.

Although the scramjet worked, the idea was shelved for nearly twenty years while NASA focused on more conventional, less expensive propulsion systems. In the 1980s, NASA joined with the Department of Defense to develop the National Aero-Space Plane as a replacement for the space shuttle. It would have been a large aircraft capable of taking off and landing from an ordinary runway. Powered at first by jet engines to take off and reach the necessary speed, ramjets would then take over and propel the aircraft to the edge of the atmosphere, after which rockets would push it into orbit. Since it required no external boosters and could take off and land almost anywhere, the aircraft would have had commercial applications and be used to transport passengers anywhere on Earth in a few hours. The project was shelved after Congress ended funding in 1994.

The research and $1.7 billion that went into developing the aircraft weren't entirely wasted. New technologies and materials—especially those capable of resisting high temperatures—originally meant for the aircraft have been used elsewhere in the modern aerospace industry.

NASA's research into new aircraft engines included the Advanced Turboprop Project, which lasted from 1976 to 1987. A turboprop uses a jet engine to drive a propeller. Turboprops are very fuel efficient and lighter in weight than a conventional jet engine. The most efficient aircraft engine ever developed, NASA's advanced turboprop saved from 30 to 50 percent on fuel while propelling aircraft to speeds of Mach 0.65 to 0.85.

Silent Flying

With concern growing over the pollution and noise accompanying air travel—especially near airports—by 1960 NASA had begun developing

According to its designers, the X-59 is as loud as a door closing.

aircraft that were quieter and more fuel efficient. Noise reduction became a real priority with the introduction of faster-than-sound aircraft. The loud boom that accompanied breaking the sound barrier rattled people's homes and sometimes broke windows.

The Concorde passenger jet underscored many of these problems. Making its first flight in 1969, the Concorde—developed by Britain and France—was the first supersonic commercial passenger jet. Flying at twice the speed of sound, it could travel from New York to London in less than three hours. But problems with the concept quickly became apparent. The enormous delta wings—needed for supersonic flight—required huge amounts of fuel at takeoff. Worse, it generated three times the toxic emissions as a conventional airliner. And then there was the boom. Even when the Concorde broke the sound barrier at 60,000 feet (18,290 m), the noise was loud enough to be heard indoors by people on the ground. These problems—as well as a fatal accident—caused the Concorde program to be canceled. The plane made its last flight in 2003.

Still, the airline industry was interested in supersonic passenger aircraft—just one without the problems that plagued the Concorde. This led NASA to create its Hyper-X program, with its primary goal to develop a scramjet-powered hypersonic plane—a plane that flies at speeds greater than five times the speed of sound—that was fuel efficient, nonpolluting, and quiet.

NASA began work on its Hyper-X program in the late 1990s and built three unpiloted X-43A research aircraft. The first two were designed to reach a speed of Mach 7 and the third Mach 10. All three of the small (12 feet [3.7 m] long, 5 feet [1.5 m] wide) test vehicles were based on lifting body technology. Not only did the shape of the aircraft contribute toward its lift, but also the flat bottom of the fuselage helped feed air into the engine.

The final flight of the X-43 took place on November 16, 2004. The unpiloted scramjet achieved a speed of Mach 9.6, or about 6,800 miles (10,943 km) per hour, setting a speed record for an air-breathing aircraft. More important, the X-43 proved the viability of the scramjet for future hypersonic air travel and for cheaper, safer methods of reaching orbit.

In the 2020s, NASA's investigations into commercial supersonic air travel resulted in the X-59, part of the agency's Quiet SuperSonic Technology program. The plan is to fly the new aircraft over select communities and then record the responses of people on the ground. NASA's hope is that the aircraft will reduce the window-rattling sonic "boom" to a mere thump by breaking up the shock wave that forms as an aircraft approaches the speed of sound. To do this, the aircraft has a long, slender, needlelike nose that takes up nearly a third of its 100-foot (33 m) length. Engineers have done everything possible to streamline the aircraft, since even the slightest protrusion could create the turbulence that causes sonic booms. Even the cockpit has been removed. Instead of windows, the X-59's pilots will rely on high-resolution cameras and monitors for navigation.

The prototype of the X-59 was rolled out in January 2024. Flight tests began that summer and will continue until 2027. If the tests are successful, it may not be long before commercial versions of the X-59 become widely available. Since the aircraft would not create a sonic boom, it could safely fly over populated areas rather than avoid them, shortening its travel distances and reducing its fuel consumption.

NASA and Safer Flying

In the 1980s, as the United States became more conscious of the need for energy conservation and the need to reduce environmental pollution, NASA created a program devoted to improving the efficiency, safety, and quality of air travel. One effort was to develop aircraft that take off and land on shorter runways, thus consuming less fuel. Improving the control systems in aircraft also contributed to efficiency and safety. NASA developed digital fly-by-wire technology that replaced traditional mechanical flight controls—which had been either operated by the pilot's own muscles or through hydraulic systems similar to the power steering and power brakes in a car—with electronic controls in which a computer controlled much of the aircraft's flight automatically.

These innovations led to the glass cockpit in the 1980s and 1990s. Until then, an airline pilot faced up to one hundred or more instruments, dials, and gauges—a lot for someone to pay attention to while flying a huge aircraft. NASA replaced these with digital displays on screens as part of the fly-by-wire system, simplifying the pilot's job while giving the pilot more information about the aircraft. Pilots were less distracted and also gained more complete knowledge of the aircraft's operation for safer flying.

Glass cockpits got their name for their digital screens, which looked like glass panels. The technology paved the way for updated smart cockpit technology that eases the workload on pilots even further.

Virtually every large aircraft built since then has employed glass cockpit technology.

With as many as one hundred thousand airline flights every day, the skies were becoming increasingly crowded—and, consequently, more dangerous. In the 1990s, NASA, in partnership with the Federal Aviation Administration (FAA), began experimenting with technology for air traffic control to make keeping track of so many aircraft simpler and safer. Ames Research Center created an air traffic control simulator called FutureFlight Central to test new systems and train air traffic controllers in their use.

Many of NASA's innovations in aviation safety, such as improvements in air traffic control, benefit other transportation systems as well. One example is NASA's solution to the danger of taking off and landing on wet or icy runways. Cutting grooves into concrete surfaces with diamond-edged blades increases traction on roads and runways, reducing hydroplaning (when tires on a wet road lose contact with the pavement) and skidding. NASA developed this initially to keep aircraft, including returning space shuttles, safe during landing, but it has since been applied to the runways of hundreds of commercial airports as well as highways, stairs, sidewalks, and parking lots. A study by the California Department of Highways noted an 85 percent decrease in accidents on wet highways that had been grooved.

Solar-Powered Flight

In searching for ways to fly without relying on energy sources that pollute the environment, NASA engineers have looked to solar power. One of the agency's innovations was Pathfinder, a remote-controlled flying wing powered entirely by the sun. NASA's goal was to come up with an aircraft that could remain in the air for weeks or even months at a time, making it ideal for gathering information and images about climate and conditions in the atmosphere and on the ground.

Pathfinder was built to demonstrate the possible use of solar power for long, high-altitude flights. The upper side of its 98-foot (30 m) wingspan was almost entirely covered with solar panels that generated 7,500 watts of power to feed the aircraft's six electric motors. Pathfinder made its first test flight on July 27, 1995, reaching an altitude of 50,500 feet (15.4 km), and in 1997 it flew up to 71,530 feet (21.8 km). It is not a fast aircraft, managing speeds of only 15 to 20 miles (24 to 32 km) per hour. But Pathfinder doesn't need to be fast. Being able to stay at such high altitudes for long periods make it ideal as a research probe. In 1998 Pathfinder was modified into the Pathfinder Plus model, which was larger and more powerful.

Even larger and more impressive yet was Pathfinder's successor Helios. Helios's solar panels powered fourteen motors mounted along the front edge of the wing. Much larger than Pathfinder, with a wingspan of 247 feet (75 m)—wider than the wingspan of a Boeing 747 airliner—the remote-controlled Helios was able to reach an altitude of nearly 100,000 feet (30.5 km) on a single-day flight in 2001 and maintained an altitude above 50,000 feet (15 km) continuously for at least four days in 2003.

The subject of solar-powered aircraft—aircraft that use no fuel—leads to the core of a great deal of NASA research: climate change and Earth's environment. In addition to its work in studying the effects of global warming (see chapter 9), NASA has been a leader in developing aircraft technology that has minimal effect on the environment.

Green Aircraft

Commercial aircraft have long had a major flaw: They are not very good for the environment. Since the invention of the airplane in 1903, aircraft engines have relied on fossil fuels. Each year aircraft burn an average of over 99 billion gallons (375 billion L) of fossil fuels. Hoping to reduce air, water, and noise pollution, in 2010 NASA completed an eighteen-month study to look into future passenger airliner designs that would be more fuel efficient, safer, and quieter than present-day aircraft. In their study, NASA investigated new materials for building aircraft that would be lighter and stronger, as well as electric propulsion, flying wings, and even replacing windows with virtual reality screens. Looking ahead to 2040, NASA envisions aircraft with zero emissions and zero impact on the environment.

Among the many experimental aircraft NASA is studying are two that it hopes will have little or no impact on the environment. The X-66A was designed to significantly reduce greenhouse gas emissions, while the X-57 is an all-electric aircraft whose engines run on rechargeable batteries.

Developed in conjunction with Boeing, the X-66A has very long, thin wings that are stabilized by diagonal struts or trusses. The shape of the wings produces less drag, allowing the plane to fly through the air with less resistance, and the trusses provide additional lift. The design uses less fuel, perhaps as much as 30 percent less, than present commercial airliners. In many ways this concept resembles the biplanes of World War I that used a pair of wings to create more lift. Based on wind tunnel test results, the full-size aircraft, expected to make its first flight in 2028 and be in commercial operation by 2035, will be able to carry passengers at speeds of up to Mach 0.80 (most commercial airliners today travel at between Mach 0.60 and 0.90).

NASA's X-57 "Maxwell" would have been one of the strangest-looking aircraft that the agency's designers ever invented. Otherwise looking like an ordinary airplane, the X-57 had fourteen electric motors and propellers: six along the leading edge of each wing, and two additional larger motors and propellers at the tips of the wings. These motors would be powered by large, rechargeable lithium-ion batteries stored behind the cockpit. The smaller motors were to be used mainly for takeoff and landing, while the two larger ones would propel the plane at cruising speed.

NASA had hoped that electric aircraft propulsion would reduce greenhouse gas emissions by five to ten times and that the first test flights would occur by 2018. But numerous technical setbacks—largely with the motors—forced NASA to delay the test flights until it eventually abandoned the X-57A program in June 2023.

NASA is not quite done with electrically propelled aircraft. The agency has joined with the US Air Force's Air Force Work Project program and the private aviation company AFWERX to develop an electric-propelled vertical takeoff and landing vehicle. It looks like a very large drone: a passenger compartment surrounded by six propellers at the end of long booms. Their main function would be as "air taxis": small aircraft used to transport small numbers of people on short flights between points not served by regular airlines.

Chapter 12

NASA and You

With a budget of $25 billion funded by American taxpayers, NASA might seem like a very expensive investment. After all, what possible personal benefit do ordinary American citizens gain from a government agency that shoots rockets to the moon and Mars?

There is scarcely any part of your daily life that has not been impacted in some way by technology or materials that came from NASA research. Beginning more than fifty years ago, the list of NASA's contributions is long, with some of its most familiar inventions including memory foam mattresses, cell phone cameras, crash helmets, cordless vacuums and power tools, emergency "space blankets" used by first responders to keep accident victims warm, implantable heart monitors, freeze-dried food, and cochlear implants that enable deaf people to hear without hearing aids. Lightweight high-temperature alloys used in jet engines, compact water purification systems, and global search and rescue systems have all benefited from NASA research. The miniaturized electronics and communications satellites that make the internet and GPS possible came from NASA developments.

Even the computer mouse originated with NASA. And while $23 billion is a huge budget, NASA actually returns more money to the economy than it gets. In 2021 NASA contributed nearly $72 billion to the national economy—that's a return of 300 percent on the taxpayer's investment in the agency. And NASA provides thousands of jobs: more than

19,000 people work directly for the agency and nearly 340,000 indirectly through the companies NASA contracts for research and manufacturing. NASA's investment in climate change research alone supports more than 37,000 jobs. NASA also invests in new companies and the development of new materials, products, and technologies. All fifty states, as well as the District of Columbia, benefit from NASA activities.

Medicine, Safety, and Health

During the COVID-19 pandemic, when thousands of critically ill people had to rely on ventilators to breathe, hospitals faced a shortage of the devices. To address the shortage, NASA engineers developed an inexpensive, simple ventilator. It used parts that were easy to obtain, so as to not compete with the manufacture of traditional ventilators. The new ventilator was made available only a little over a month after work on it had begun, saving many lives.

Other NASA engineers had been working on a human-powered ventilator, one that did not depend on an outside power source, for use in spacecraft. They realized this would be ideal for COVID-19 patients waiting for a powered ventilator to become available or for use in underdeveloped countries where power might be unreliable. Other NASA engineers worked with private companies to develop devices that would effectively create a fine, antimicrobial mist that could eliminate the COVID virus from the air and from surfaces.

In its search for life in the solar system, NASA is very interested in studying organisms that survive in extreme conditions, such as those that might be found on Mars, Europa, or Titan. NASA scientists began examining the microorganisms that flourish in the boiling temperatures of Yellowstone's hot springs and discovered a microbe that might be a source of protein for astronauts on long space missions to Mars. Requiring less water and land than is needed to raise beef, this new food source has less impact on the environment than traditional cattle farming, and astronauts could easily grow it aboard a spacecraft. Already the protein has found its way into grocery stores as vegan breakfast patties and nondairy cream cheese.

The Boy in the Bubble

NASA was helping to save lives as early as 1977. David Vetter was a six-year-old boy suffering from an immune deficiency disease. His body wasn't able to fight off infections. Even the slightest cold was potentially dangerous and could be fatal. Since birth he had to be confined to a series of isolators—sealed, germproof plastic bubbles—at Texas Children's Hospital. To help David get around, NASA presented him with a special system that resembled a bright yellow, miniature space suit. It allowed him to take walks and interact freely with his family and friends for the first time in his life. The suit was attached to a portable life-support system that filtered the air David breathed.

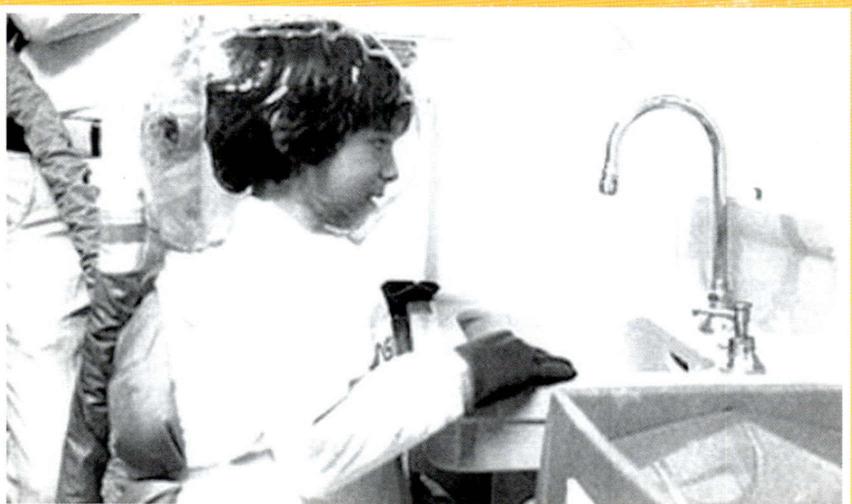

David Vetter

Other innovations in the health, medical, and safety sectors include the following:

Cataract surgery. Instruments developed to fine-tune the James Webb Space Telescope led to improvements in LASIK eye surgery, used to correct vision problems including nearsightedness and farsightedness. The doctor once had to rely on the measurements provided by the patient's own eyeglasses. The new technology makes more than twelve hundred detailed measurements directly of the eyes, for safer, more accurate results.

Cancer treatments. Scientists working aboard the space shuttle developed a method to boost plant growth by using pinhead-sized light-emitting diodes (LEDs). Researchers at NASA's Marshall Space Flight Center have used this technology in the treatment of cancer. Doctors inject a patient with a light-sensitive, cancer-treating drug. The drug is activated by tiny LEDs that can be focused on very small areas of the patient's body, enabling the drug to destroy cancer cells while leaving the surrounding tissue untouched.

Firefighter equipment. Much of the safety equipment used by firefighters throughout the United States uses lightweight materials NASA developed for the US space program. Breathing equipment, fire-resistant fabrics, and handheld ultraviolet fire detectors used by firefighters also came from NASA research.

Environmental cleanup. NASA efforts to prevent pollutants from damaging the environment around launch sites have led to innovations in cleanup technology that have been used to save polluted wetlands around the world.

Energy

The need to provide reliable, compact sources of power for spacecraft has led NASA to develop materials and techniques that are now used in everyday life. Solar cells and fuel cells are two of these innovations. The solar cell produces energy directly from sunlight. The fuel cell generates electricity directly from the combination of a fuel, such as hydrogen, and oxygen. NASA has been using fuel cells for almost all of its human space missions since the Gemini program. They are relatively simple devices and a clean energy source with little impact on the environment, producing only electricity, water vapor, and heat. The water vapor can be broken down again into hydrogen and oxygen and reused. Fuel cells are ideal for places too remote or undeveloped to have regular electrical service.

NASA has also been using solar energy to power spacecraft for decades. Because weight and simplicity are important considerations in space travel,

NASA has developed solar panels that are lightweight and efficient. While the manufacture of solar panels consumes large amounts of energy and water and requires the mining of potentially hazardous metals such as selenium, silicon, and copper, it is also a relatively easy and inexpensive process. Since solar panels emit no greenhouse gases, they have little impact on the environment once in use, and in recent years, as solar panels have become more popular, manufacturers have started to use more recycled and recyclable materials. NASA has already created an airplane powered entirely by solar energy and believes that its new panels might be used to power not only charging stations for electric vehicles but also cars and trucks that would carry similar solar panels.

Communications

All of us take advantage of NASA communication technology every day: the weather reports we get from space, talking with friends and sharing photos on our smartphones, and watching high-definition television shows broadcast from around the world. Each of these activities is made possible by satellites beaming information to Earth.

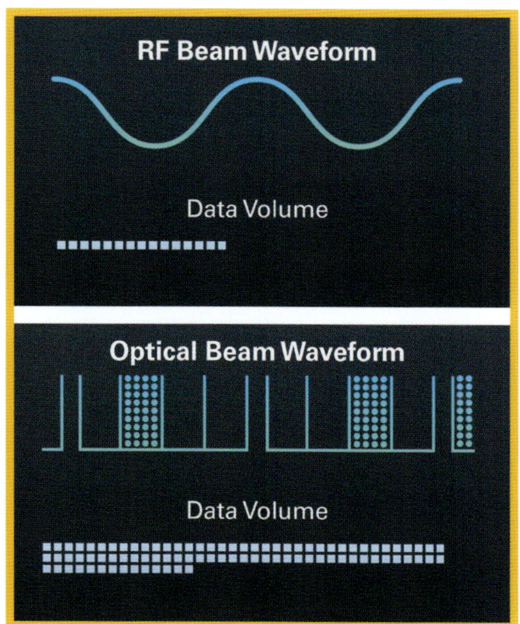

This diagram shows how more data can be packed into an optical laser beam (*bottom*) than a radio wave (*top*).

NASA's contributions to communications go back to 1962, when it launched the first Telstar satellite. Telstar, a joint project between NASA and the communications company AT&T, was the first commercial satellite. Its purpose was to relay signals from one ground station to another thousands of miles away. Until then, the only way to transmit television and telephone signals was by linking stations together directly by a series of towers or by cables. The Telstar satellites relayed the first transcontinental television pictures and telephone calls as well as the first live transatlantic television broadcast. Since then, more than twenty Telstar satellites have been placed in orbit; the last was launched in 2018.

Since its contributions to worldwide radio broadcast networks, NASA has begun investigating communicating with higher energy beams of light. The agency has found that using lasers instead of radio waves for communication enables ten to one hundred times more data to be transmitted in the same amount of time. Lasers are also smaller, lighter, and use less power than radios. One day we may all be using ultra-high-speed laser communications instead of radio.

Robotics

All of NASA's probes to other planets have been robots, including the rovers sent to Mars. In addition to performing tasks and collecting scientific data and samples, robots are necessary for space exploration for a simple reason: distance. For instance, because Mars is so far away from Earth, there is a five- to ten-minute delay between when NASA sends a signal to a rover on the surface and when it arrives—which becomes ten to twenty minutes between sending a signal and receiving a reply. If a rover is heading into a situation where it might be damaged or lost, the accident likely will have occurred long before an operator on Earth could respond. This means that NASA's Mars rovers need to be able to make their own decisions. With future plans to explore not only Mars but also Earth's moon, asteroids, and Jupiter's moon Europa, rovers need to be able to deal with obstacles such as cliffs, steep hills, and icy terrain.

The programming and technology used in NASA's Mars rovers has practical applications here on Earth. Able to navigate any sort of terrain and endure conditions that might be too dangerous for humans, earthbound NASA robots are used by scientists exploring inaccessible regions on Earth, firefighters, law enforcement, and rescue teams in your hometown.

These experimental robots have taken many, often unusual, forms:

NASA scientists test out the EELS robot in an environment similar to that of Enceladus.

- The Limbed Excursion Mechanical Utility Robot has four leglike limbs with sixteen fingers on each. The fingers are equipped with tiny hooks, allowing the robot to climb nearly vertical walls.
- Resembling a mechanical snake, Exobiology Extant Life Surveyor, called EELS, is well named. Designed to explore the narrow, geyserlike vents on Saturn's moon Enceladus, EELS can wriggle its way into narrow cracks and crevices.
- The Rollocopter can roll over a landscape on a pair of large wheels, but if it comes to an obstacle it can't get past, it flies over it, using four dronelike propellers.
- The Legged Locomotion and Movement Adaptation resembles a llama, the four-legged animal it is named for. Llamas live in the Andes mountains of Peru and are known for their agility in navigating rocky terrain. This robot has an advantage over other robots in that it can move very quickly in any direction.

As NASA develops new robots to deal with the strange environments found on other worlds in our solar system, new applications for these robots will continue to be found here on Earth.

Chapter 13

The Future of NASA

NASA has a busy future ahead. In addition to further robotic probes to the planets and their moons and more space telescopes, NASA hopes to send humans to both the moon and Mars in coming years. And NASA is working on technology with the potential to send probes to other stars.

Working Together

NASA has always partnered with private contractors and companies to oversee some of the design and manufacturing of aircraft, spacecraft, and other technologies and devices. These partnerships have aided the development and building of all of NASA's spacecraft—from Mercury to the space shuttle. Collaborating with private companies allows NASA to explore a range of solutions and innovate in areas it otherwise couldn't. In 1979 NASA released guidelines for the increased use of its publicly funded resources by the private sector. The goal was to achieve "domestic commercial exploitation of space capabilities, technology, and systems for national economic benefit," and the government would "provide a climate conducive to expanded private sector investment and involvement in space activities." Companies such as SpaceX, Blue Origin, Virgin Galactic, and others have been developing their own launch vehicles and spacecraft. For many of these projects, NASA provides technical information, launch facilities, and ground support. However, some critics believe NASA gives too much in public funds to these private companies without getting enough in return.

Twice a year, NASA permits private businesses to use their own spacecraft to transport engineers and scientists to the International Space Station. Once there, these researchers can conduct experiments and perform activities for up to two weeks. The first of these private missions was conducted in 2022 by the company Axiom Space.

Retiring the Space Shuttle

As the twenty-first century approached, NASA realized that the space shuttle had served its purpose. One of its main functions, supplying modules and other components for the International Space Station, would be no longer needed once the ISS was complete. Using the space shuttle solely to transport personnel to and from the station was inefficient and expensive. It was a very large spacecraft for carrying a maximum of only eight people to orbit. The average cost for a space shuttle launch was $450 million. It was like using a moving van to deliver a postcard.

Following the Columbia disaster in 2003, President George W. Bush formally announced that the Space Shuttle program would be retired after the completion of the ISS. To replace the program, NASA announced an ambitious new program in 2004 called Constellation. This program had three main goals. First, to develop a new heavy booster to replace the space shuttle in sending cargo and personnel to the ISS, as well as to launch other spacecraft and satellites. Second, to return humans to the moon and to establish a permanent outpost there. Third, the human exploration of Mars.

In addition to the new heavy boosters, a core component of the Constellation program is the Orion spacecraft. Resembling an enlarged version of the Apollo Command Module, it can ferry up to four passengers to and from the ISS. Equipped with four large solar panels, it could remain in space for up to twenty-one days, more than enough time for a round trip to the moon.

The Constellation program eventually ran too far over budget and behind schedule. The cost of continuing the program came in at over

$15 billion, an investment too high for Congress. Meanwhile, several private companies, such as SpaceX and Blue Origins, had been developing their own heavy-lift boosters. This took some of the burden off NASA to develop similar launch vehicles of its own. The Constellation program was officially canceled in 2010. Since then, rockets developed by SpaceX and other companies have transported personnel and supplies to the ISS. Meanwhile, NASA continued work on the Orion module, which became a core component of a new program: Artemis.

Back to the Moon: Artemis

In 2017 NASA officially announced its new plan to return to the moon. The agency named the lunar landing program Artemis. In ancient Greek mythology, Artemis was not only a goddess of the moon but also the twin sister of Apollo: a perfect choice for the name of the first human missions to the moon in more than fifty years.

The Space Launch System is the only rocket powerful enough to send Orion, astronauts, and cargo to the moon in one trip.

The mission depends on the giant Space Launch System booster, the most powerful rocket ever built. At a towering 322 feet (98 m), it is taller than the Statue of Liberty. It will have 13 percent more thrust than the space shuttle and 15 percent more than the Saturn 5 that took the Apollo astronauts to the moon. Its first launch was on November 16, 2022, when NASA sent the uncrewed Artemis 1 spacecraft on a million-mile (1.6 million km) trip around the moon.

Artemis 2, scheduled for launch in 2026, will send a crew of four on a journey to the moon: Commander Reid Wiseman, pilot Victor Glover (the first person of color to leave low Earth orbit),

NASA Mission Specialist Christina Koch (the first woman to do so), and Canadian Space Agency astronaut Jeremy Hansen (the first non-American to do so). They will circle the moon before returning to Earth. The success of this mission will lay the groundwork for Artemis 3, which will land near the south pole of the moon in 2026.

A Base on the Moon

Future Artemis missions to the moon will be in several stages. First, the astronauts travel from Earth to the moon in an Orion spacecraft. Then, they board the Gateway space station, which will be in orbit around the moon. Like the ISS, the Gateway station will be an international project between NASA and space agencies from Europe, Japan, Canada, and the United Arab Emirates. It will consist of several modules, including a living space, a laboratory, solar power panels, and the docked Orion spacecraft.

Next, astronauts have to establish the Artemis Base Camp on the surface of the moon. Gateway will function like a bus or train station, where the astronauts transfer from the Orion spacecraft that carried them from Earth to a Human Landing System that takes them down to the surface of the moon. Meanwhile, the astronauts already working aboard Gateway (which is meant to remain in orbit for at least fifteen years) will perform experiments and take observations of the moon.

The Artemis Base Camp will be near the lunar south pole. One of the reasons scientists chose this site is that the astronauts will have access to the water ice that has been found there. The ice will be not only a source of water for drinking but also for the manufacture of oxygen for breathing and rocket fuel.

NASA has planned the first missions to stay at the Artemis Base Camp for only a few days, but as the project grows, crews of as many as four astronauts may stay for up to two months at a time, embarking on weeklong expeditions across the lunar surface using two new transportation systems. The first of these vehicles is the Lunar Terrain Vehicle, similar to the rover the earlier Apollo astronauts used. It will have a traveling range of around 12 miles (19 km) on a single charge. The vehicle can be driven remotely by the crew in the Artemis Base Camp or from Earth. In addition, the astronauts will have a rover with a pressurized cabin called a habitable mobility platform, much like a small spaceship on wheels that will enable astronauts to travel across the moon in regular working clothes. It would provide breathable air and protection against heat, cold, and radiation. They will need to put on their space suits only when they leave the vehicle.

Several different aerospace companies are developing designs for both vehicles. The Orion capsule was successfully tested on December 5, 2014, when it made an uncrewed orbit around the moon, returning to Earth safely two orbits and four hours later.

From Earth to Mars

NASA hopes to send humans to Mars by the 2030s. A round trip to the planet would entail a journey of 1.2 to 1.8 billion miles (1.9 to 2.9 billion km)—nearly a thousand times as far as a round trip to the moon. Because Mars's orbit around the sun is a little longer than Earth's, the distance between the two planets constantly changes. NASA plans to send the astronauts to Mars when that distance is the shortest. Once on Mars, the astronauts will wait until Earth and Mars line up again for the shortest journey back home, which happens about every two years. This means the mission may take as long as one thousand days, three hundred of which would need to be spent on Mars. Even the shortest possible mission has astronauts spending more than a year in space.

NASA has had a lot of experience providing life support for long-term missions in space. More than 220 astronauts have lived aboard the ISS since 2000, with one astronaut living in the station for more than a year. Nevertheless, a journey to Mars presents many challenges for the survival of its human astronauts. They will need five essential elements to survive: air, water, food, energy, and shelter. It is almost impossible to carry enough food, air, and water for such a long journey. The astronauts would have to create their own. The life-support systems on the spacecraft will have to recycle at least 98 percent of water consumed and 75 percent of oxygen from the carbon dioxide that astronauts exhale. Food might be grown aboard the spacecraft and in the landing module on Mars. Studies conducted on the ISS have shown that growing plants in space is possible.

While on Mars, oxygen for the explorers might be generated from the Martian atmosphere, from minerals in its soil, or from ice. Recycled water might be combined with water derived from Martian ice.

NASA's human Mars missions are deep in their planning stages. Many decisions still have to be made: What sort of spacecraft will make the trip? What sort of propulsion will it use? How will the astronauts live while on Mars? Answers to these questions apply not only to traveling to Mars but also to the future exploration of the solar system. Just as humans never stop exploring our own planet, once we have visited Mars, we will inevitably look to farther destinations.

Looking for Life

The search for life—even if only signs of ancient life, such as fossils—has been a driving force behind many of NASA's missions. All its probes to comets and asteroids have searched for traces of water and organic compounds, and every orbiter, lander, and rover to visit Mars has looked for evidence of life, whether present or past. Finding signs of life elsewhere in the solar system would provide valuable information about our own origins on Earth as well as how common life is across the universe, similar to how scientists learn about the human body by using comparative anatomy. By learning how animals evolved and comparing their bodies to those of humans, scientists can theorize how humans evolved and learn more about how our bodies work. Discovering life on a world like Mars or Titan might be like getting a glimpse into our own planet's distant past when life first formed here. Seeing how life might have evolved to cope with the extreme environments found on other worlds will tell us much about how evolution works. And we might learn about the future of life on our own planet as its environment changes.

At least three of NASA's future missions plan on searching for life in the most promising places.

EUROPA

Life needs three basic ingredients: liquid water; a source of elements such as carbon, nitrogen, phosphorus, and sulfur; and a source of energy. Europa, a moon of Jupiter, likely has all of these. Europa is covered entirely in a mantle of ice between 10 to 15 miles (15 to 25 km) thick. NASA's earlier Galileo mission to Jupiter found that vast, salty oceans might lie beneath this icy crust, and some scientists believe the moon—with the exception of a small, rocky core—is mostly water. If that is true, Europa contains nearly twice as much water as all of the oceans and lakes on Earth combined. Many scientists believe that these oceans may contain the organic compounds on which life is based. One of Europa's sources of energy includes the heat created by tidal flexing, an effect of Jupiter's gravity.

The goal of NASA's Europa Clipper is to confirm these ideas and make new discoveries about this mysterious moon. NASA launched Europa Clipper on October 14, 2024. Large enough to span the length of a basketball court, Europa Clipper is the largest spacecraft meant to explore another world that NASA has ever launched. It is due to arrive at Jupiter in 2030 after a journey of 1.8 billion miles (2.9 billion km). Once there, it will go into an orbit around Jupiter that will take it close to Jupiter's large icy moon, Europa, forty-nine times. It will get as close as 16 miles (26 km) to the moon. Each time it does a flyby, it will scan a different area of the moon until, when the mission is complete, it will have photographed and studied virtually the entire surface.

Instruments aboard Europa Clipper will study Europa's thin atmosphere, while radar will penetrate the ice to search for water. Other instruments will scan for areas of warmer ice on the surface that might indicate subsurface water and perhaps recent geyserlike eruptions. These instruments will measure the thickness of Europa's ice, determine its composition, and explore the surface geology of the moon.

NASA plans to follow up Europa Clipper with the Europa Lander. A drill-like probe would collect samples from about 4 inches (10 cm) beneath the ice. This is deep enough for the ice to have been able to protect any complex organic molecules from the intense radiation emitted by Jupiter. A miniature laboratory—similar to the one on the Viking Mars landers—will then study the samples to learn their composition and to see if any of the chemicals found indicate the presence of life. The Europa Lander also would take close-up photos of the landscape and examine the surface and samples with a microscope. A seismometer will look for signs of the ice shifting, like floes in Earth's Arctic, or eruptions of ice geysers.

NASA scientists sometimes test equipment on Earth in environments similar to those astronauts might find on another planet or moon. These experiments help them plan for real space missions.

TITAN

In addition to Jupiter, Saturn has two moons that have intrigued NASA scientists looking for signs of life in the solar system, Titan and Enceladus.

In 1997 the European Space Agency's Huygens probe hitched a ride aboard NASA's Cassini spacecraft, headed for Saturn. Arriving in 2005, Huygens separated from the main spacecraft and made a safe landing on Titan. Until then, the giant moon had been a mystery. It's the only moon in the solar system with a dense atmosphere. Thick orange clouds hide its surface from Earth-based observers, so no one knew what might be there.

The Huygens lander found a cold world (Titan is ten times farther away from the sun than Earth is), with a surface temperature of −290°F (−179°C). Because Titan's atmosphere is so dense, air pressure at the surface is half again greater than Earth's. Titan's atmosphere is mostly nitrogen, but with large amounts of methane, an organic hydrocarbon (a molecule of carbon and hydrogen); it falls like rain and collects in pools and lakes. Other organic compounds continually fall from the heavy clouds, covering the landscape in a blanket of orange snow. Despite the low temperature, Titan has all the ingredients for the formation of life: water, organic molecules, and a source of energy.

In 2028 NASA will launch a new mission to Titan: Dragonfly, a flying drone equipped with eight rotors. Arriving in 2036, Dragonfly will explore

Titan for the next 2.7 years, flying more than 108 miles (174 km) as it looks for water, complex organic compounds, and perhaps signs that life may once have evolved on the giant moon—or that life may still exist there.

ENCELADUS

Saturn's other moon that interests scientists looking for life in the solar system is Enceladus. It is one of the handful of worlds in our solar system known to have a subsurface ocean of liquid water. Scientists didn't have to guess at this: Enceladus made it obvious. Huge geysers of water vapor are constantly erupting from vents near Enceladus's south pole, ejecting feathery plumes hundreds of miles into space. Samples of the water vapor taken by the Cassini orbiter have shown that deep beneath the icy crust of the moon are most of the chemical ingredients needed for life.

NASA's future Enceladus Vent Explorer will consist of a two-part spacecraft. A lander will set down within a few hundred feet of an erupting vent. One or more rovers will then move to the vent and attempt to descend into it. This will be a tricky operation since the material ejecting from the vent might be traveling as fast as 800 miles (1,287 km) per hour, faster than the exhaust of a jet engine. Instruments aboard the rovers will then take samples and make detailed measurements of the composition of the geysers.

Space Tourism

The idea of visiting space excites many people—including those who train to become astronauts. Although the majority of people who go beyond Earth's orbit are scientists and astronauts, several private companies, such as Blue Origins and Virgin Galactic, offer "tours" of space to ordinary citizens. They launch suborbital flights into space, which give space tourists a few minutes in space before their spacecraft returns to Earth. Longer trips into space—a few weeks at a space station or, in the more distant future, trips to the moon or Mars—require further considerations of both cost and safety. But more than sixty years of successful spaceflight have helped to lower the costs of space travel. The expensive boosters and external tanks used by the space shuttles were lost after every launch, while the Falcon Heavy booster used by SpaceX is almost entirely recycled. It cost up to $30,000 for the space shuttle to send 1 pound (0.5 kg) to orbit, but the Falcon Heavy can launch the same amount of cargo for just $700.

Safety is another issue. For short trips into space—up to two weeks—the effects of radiation and microgravity are minimal. But a trip to Mars would require months in space. To prevent passengers from experiencing muscle and bone density loss, the spacecraft would have to rotate to produce artificial gravity—a task entailing complex engineering problems that scientists have yet to solve. And to protect a tourist from the radiation they would be exposed to for such a long time requires the spacecraft to be covered in heavy shielding. Anything that adds weight to a spacecraft adds to the fuel requirements, and thus increases the costs.

While it may be a while before space tourism companies can offer longer trips, advancements on the science side of space exploration help bring the possibility closer to reality.

The Distant Future

NASA's Innovative Advanced Concepts program looks to the future—sometimes the far distant future—to generate ideas for space exploration. One of the focuses of the program is propulsion. The faster and cheaper a spacecraft can travel, the sooner humans will be able to explore Mars and the outer planets. With existing technology, it takes more than nine months to make a one-way trip to Mars. New Horizons, the fastest spacecraft to ever leave Earth, took fourteen years to reach Pluto. The Innovative Advanced Concepts program has looked at many potential ways to make space travel faster, safer, and cheaper. The following are just a few:

NUCLEAR THERMAL PROPULSION

NASA research into using nuclear energy directly for propelling spacecraft began in the early 1960s, though the idea had been around for a lot longer. The program was called Nuclear Engine for Rocket Vehicle Application. The idea was fairly simple: Use the heat generated by a nuclear reactor to bring hydrogen to a very high temperature. The hydrogen then exhausts through a nozzle, propelling the spacecraft. A nuclear rocket could be two or three times more efficient than a rocket burning chemical fuels and likely would also be much faster, permitting much shorter travel times to the moon and other planets. But nuclear propulsion presents some potential dangers. One is that the hydrogen exhaust will probably have been made radioactive by passing through the reactor. Another is the possibility that an accident might release radioactive material into the atmosphere. For these reasons, a nuclear-powered spacecraft would have to operate only in the vacuum of space. It would be used to travel between planets, while ordinary chemical rockets would be used to transfer personnel, supplies, and equipment to and from the surface of Earth or another planet.

NASA is developing the Demonstration Rocket for Agile Cislunar Operations program to test a nuclear-powered spacecraft by 2027. If successful, a rocket using similar propulsion could transport humans to Mars in forty-five days instead of more than half a year.

ELECTRIC/ION PROPULSION

An electric propulsion system uses electricity provided by either solar panels or a nuclear reactor to ionize an inert gas (a gas that doesn't react with other elements) such as xenon or krypton. The ionized gas is then passed into a thruster that contains a grid with the same electric charge as the gas. As the gas passes through the grid, it is repelled by the grid's charge, which pushes it out of the thruster at a very high speed. The amount of thrust is very low—just a few pounds compared to the tons of thrust a chemical rocket might produce. A chemical rocket uses up its fuel very quickly, though, while the ion rocket can run for months or even years at a time, going faster and faster.

NASA launched the Dawn mission to the asteroids Vesta and Ceres from Earth using an ordinary chemical booster, but once the probe was in space, it used an ion thruster. When it arrived at Vesta, the probe swung around 180 degrees and used the thruster to slow down. After orbiting the asteroid for a year, it fired up its thruster and traveled to Ceres, where it remains. Maneuvers like these would have been difficult, time-consuming, and expensive with ordinary chemical rockets.

SOLAR SAILING

Light exerts pressure when it falls onto a surface. If you think this pressure

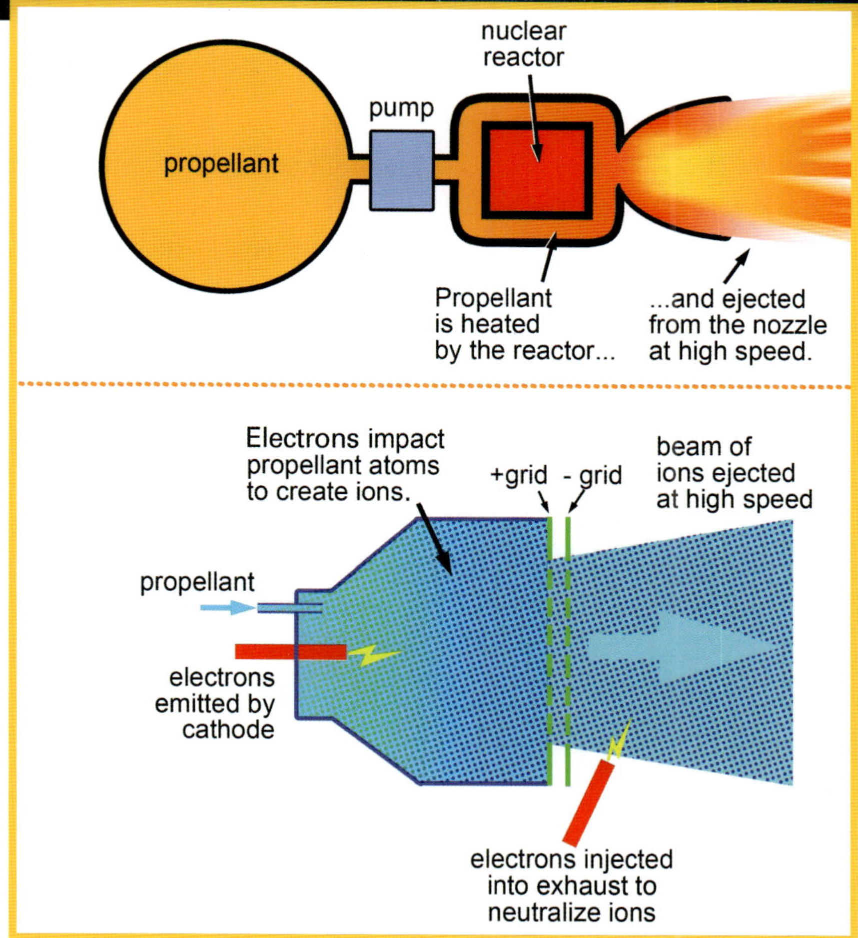

These diagrams illustrate how nuclear rockets (*top*) and ion propulsion systems (*bottom*) work.

is not very much, you would be right. The force of sunlight falling on 1 square inch is just 0.00000000065 pounds (0.000000000046 kg per sq. cm)—far too small a force for humans to feel. But if the light were to hit a large enough surface, this tiny force would add up to a lot. This is the idea behind the solar sail. If a sail could be made large enough—hundreds or even thousands of square feet—and of a light enough material, sunlight would propel it through space just as wind lifts a kite or propels a sailboat. The main advantage of a solar sail is that it uses no fuel. And if left alone to accelerate under the pressure of sunlight, it is capable of reaching very high speeds.

NASA tested a model solar sail in 2010. It was about 108 square feet (10 sq. m) of very thin plastic deployed from a CubeSat. Although it was orbiting rather close to Earth and was affected by traces of Earth's atmosphere, its gravity, and other factors, the sail did demonstrate the effect of solar radiation during the 240 days it was in orbit.

Another solar sail test, NASA's Advanced Composite Solar Sail System, is scheduled to launch into Earth orbit in 2024. This sail will be about 860 square feet (80 sq. m) and is a scaled-down prototype of a much larger future solar sail spacecraft that will measure roughly 5,400 square feet (500 sq. m). It is made of new materials that NASA hopes will be more effective as a solar sail.

One idea that might be possible with future technology would be to give a solar sail its initial push by focusing powerful orbiting or moon-based lasers onto it. The lasers could accelerate a solar sail up to 20 percent of the speed of light (37,500 miles [60,350 km] per second). Then it could reach Proxima Centauri, the nearest star, in just twenty years.

THE E-SAIL

Instead of being propelled by light, the electric sail, or E-sail, would be propelled by the solar wind—a constant stream of positively charged particles ejected by the sun. One NASA E-sail concept consists of a small central spacecraft that would spin and deploy twenty thin, positively charged wires that are each 12 miles (20 km) long. Electric charges that are the same repel one another, so when the positively charged protons from the solar wind reach the positively charged wires, they are repelled, giving the sail a push. One advantage of this technique is that E-sails might be faster than ordinary solar sails and would probably be much easier to build.

PELLET-BEAM PROPULSION

Pellet-beam propulsion requires two spacecraft. One remains orbiting Earth. The other is destined to travel to Mars or another planet. As the second vehicle departs, the homebound orbiter fires a continuous series of tiny, metallic pellets at it. At the same time, it fires a powerful laser at the pellets. The laser beam heats the pellets and partially vaporizes them into plasma, a superhot cloud of ionized particles. The burst of plasma accelerates each pellet—as though each one had a little rocket motor attached—and when the pellets strike a special target on the departing spacecraft, they transfer energy to it, making it go faster. It's a little like making something move by aiming a garden hose at it.

The Innovative Advanced Concepts program doesn't limit itself just to advanced propulsion systems. Almost any aspect of space exploration interests the program. Among its projects include studies on how to prepare Martian soil for agriculture, new techniques for coming closer to the sun than the Parker probe did, methods of creating new types of giant orbiting telescopes, figuring out how to derive fuel from materials found on icy moons, using 3D printers to create habitats on the moon and Mars, and even exploring the possibility of creating soil on asteroids by seeding them with fungi.

Where Does NASA Go from Here?

As NASA continues to innovate in all areas of science, from rocketry to climate monitoring, its research will benefit everyone. It is a pioneer of scientific development, working to uncover the answers to the mysteries of our universe. Humans have long looked up at the stars and wondered what was out there. Without NASA's contributions, our understanding of our place in the universe would be less complete. Its record of discovery provides inspiration and excitement for what is to come. NASA says:

> *NASA's future will continue to be a story of human exploration, technology, and science. We will go back to the Moon to learn more about what it will take to support human exploration to Mars and beyond. We will continue to nurture the development of a vibrant low-Earth orbit economy that builds on the work done to date by the International Space Station. NASA engineers will develop new technologies to improve air transport at home and meet the challenges of advanced space exploration. Our scientists will work to increase an understanding of our planet and our place in the universe. We will continue to try to answer the question, "Are we alone?"*

GLOSSARY

ablation: when heat is carried away from a surface by having layers of the surface peel away

ballistic: following an arclike path, similar to a ball thrown into the air

biosphere: that region of Earth, including its surface, oceans, and atmosphere, that contains life

booster: a large rocket used to launch a smaller rocket or satellite into orbit

centrifugal force: the force on an object traveling along a circular path that keeps the object moving on the path

contact binary: two bodies, such as two asteroids, that touch each other

CubeSat: a small satellite built to a standard size

drag: the forces, such as air resistance, that oppose the movement of an aircraft through the air

flyby: a close approach by a spacecraft to a moon or planet without going into orbit

gravitational assist: using a close approach to a planet to add speed and a change of direction to a spacecraft

heliopause: the boundary where the solar wind from the sun meets the interstellar medium

heliosphere: the region around the sun affected by the solar wind

ion: an atom with an electric charge

Kuiper Belt: a region of icy bodies surrounding the solar system beyond the orbit of Neptune

lift: the force, usually created by the wings, that opposes the weight of an airplane and supports it in the air

lifting body: an aircraft specially shaped so that its body provides lift instead of wings

microgravity: a condition of very low gravity

orbit: the ellipse-shaped path a moon, planet, or satellite takes when traveling around another body

oxidizer: a substance that adds oxygen to rocket fuel and allows it to combust

photochemistry: chemical reactions triggered by high-energy light

plasma: matter superheated to such a high temperature that electrons are stripped from its atoms, resulting in an ionized gas

rover: a robotic explorer equipped with motorized wheels for exploring the surface of a moon or planet

satellite: a small body orbiting a larger one

solar wind: a stream of charged particles flowing in all directions from the sun

space station: a permanent or semipermanent satellite with a crew aboard

suborbital: the path of a spacecraft that reaches outer space but does not attain orbit

thrust: the amount of pushing power of a rocket engine, measured in pounds or tons

wind tunnel: a large tube with air moving through it, used to study the actions of an object in flight

SOURCE NOTES

4 "could not help . . . awe and admiration": "On November 21, 1783, Benjamin Franklin . . ." The Franklin Institute, Facebook post, November 21, 2018, https://www.facebook.com/TheFranklinInstitute/posts/on-november-21-1783-benjamin-franklin-witnessed-the-first-manned-hot-air-balloon/10156710221019030/.

8 "to supervise and . . . their practical solution": James R. Hansen, "Engineering Science and the Development of the NACA Low-Drag Engine Cowling," in *From Engineering Science to Big Science,* accessed March 2, 2024, https://www.nasa.gov/history/SP-4219/Chapter1.html.

17 "orange": William R. Shelton, *Man's Conquest of Space* (National Geographic Society, 1968), 12.

17 "it became popular . . . science and technology": Shelton.

17, 19 "The present National . . . on our future.": Walter B. Hendrickson Jr., *Winging into Space* (Bobbs-Merrill, 1965), 65.

23 "is central to . . . organizations and individuals": "Minorities in Science," NASA, accessed October 20, 2023, https://www.nasa.gov/minorities-in-science/.

24 "The engineers admit . . . than they could.": National Women's History Museum, "The Women of NASA," Google Arts and Culture, accessed October 20, 2023, https://artsandculture.google.com/story/the-women-of-nasa-national-women%E2%80%99s-history-museum/lgVRUJbEpG1iIQ?hl=en.

25 "You tell me . . . to take off.": National Women's History Museum.

27 "so women's potential . . . not a Russian": Jerrie Cobb, *Woman into Space* (Prentice-Hall, 1963), 203.

27 "strongly urge immediate . . . as national goal": Cobb, 219.

28 "we seek, only . . . future without discrimination": Jess Romeo, "How the Mercury 13 Fought to Get Women in Space," JSTOR, October 1, 2020, https://daily.jstor.org/how-the-mercury-13-fought-to-get-women-in-space/.

28 "men go off . . . our social order": Romeo.

29 "before this decade is out": Shelton, *Man's Conquest,* 22.

34 "the vast loneliness . . . the good Earth": David R. Williams, "The Apollo 8 Christmas Eve Broadcast," NASA Goddard Space Flight Center, accessed October 21, 2023, https://nssdc.gsfc.nasa.gov/planetary/lunar/apollo8_xmas.html.

35 "very good": Robert Godwin, *Apollo 8: The NASA Mission Reports* (Apogee, 1999), 220.

36 "Tranquility Base here . . . Eagle has landed.": "Apollo 11 Technical Air-to-Ground Voice Transcription," NASA, accessed September 30, 2024, https://www.nasa.gov/wp-content/uploads/static/history/alsj/a11/AS11_TEC.PDF.

36 "That's one small . . . leap for mankind.": "Apollo 11."

36 "Here men from . . . for all mankind.": "Apollo 11."

43 "the flying bathtub": Giles Lambertson, "Flying Bathtubs Sell Like Hotcakes," Smithsonian, November 2010, https://www.smithsonianmag.com/air-space-magazine/flying-bathtubs-sell-like-hotcakes-57261970/.

52 "will return the . . . International Space Station": "President Bush Announces New Vision for Space Exploration Program," White House, January 14, 2004, https://georgewbush-whitehouse.archives.gov/news/releases/2004/01/20040114-3.html.

52 "in 2010, the . . . retired from service": "President Bush."

98 "help give us . . . worldwide weather observation": "Celebrating 61 Years of Watching Weather from Space," NOAA, April 1, 2021, https://www.nesdis.noaa.gov/news/celebrating-61-years-of-watching-weather-space.

99 "It was like . . . over the globe.": Jenny Marder, "The World According to Weather Satellites," NOAA/NASA, accessed March 3, 2024, https://storymaps.arcgis.com/stories/3ed6b70ffa80447aac3fcb1d3378884a.

100 "provide in-depth scientific . . . policy decision making": Michael D. King, ed., "EOS Science Plan," NASA, January 1999, https://eospso.nasa.gov/sites/default/files/publications/SciencePlan.pdf.

100 "it was also . . . of air quality": King.

109 "At NASA, our . . . on the sky.": Claire A. O'Shea, "Next Generation Experimental Aircraft Becomes NASA's Newest X-Plane," NASA, June 12, 2023, https://www.nasa.gov/news-release/next-generation-experimental-aircraft-becomes-nasas-newest-x-plane/.

126 "domestic commercial exploitation . . . in space activities": Judy Rumerman, *NASA Historical Data Book, Volume 6* (NASA, 1999), 357.

139 "NASA's future will . . . 'Are we alone?' ":"The Future," 60 Years and Counting, NASA, accessed November 16, 2023, https://www.nasa.gov/specials/60counting/future.html.

SELECTED BIBLIOGRAPHY

Anderson, Frank. *Orders of Magnitude.* NASA, 1976.

Billings, Linda. *Fifty Years of Solar System Exploration.* NASA, 2012.

Canby, Thomas. *Skylab, Outpost on the Frontier of Space.* National Geographic Society, 1974.

Carpenter, M. Scott, L. Gordon Cooper Jr., John H. Glenn Jr., Virgil I. Grissom, Walter M. Schirra Jr., Alan B. Shepard Jr., and Donald K. Slayton. *We Seven.* Simon and Schuster, 1962.

Cobb, Jerrie. *Woman into Space.* Prentice-Hall, 1963.

Crouch, Tom. *Aiming for the Stars.* Smithsonian Institution, 1999.

Fimmel, Richard O., William Swindell, and Eric Burgess. *Pioneer Odyssey: Encounter with a Giant.* NASA, 1974.

Fowler, Eugene. *One Small Step.* Smithmark, 1999.

French, Bevan M. *Mars: The Viking Discoveries.* NASA, 1977.

Gatland, Kenneth, ed. *Illustrated Encyclopedia of Space Technology.* Orion, 1989.

Hacker, Barton C., and James M. Grimwood. *On the Shoulders of Titans.* NASA, 1977.

Hallion, Richard, and Art Neff. *Forty Years of Supersonic Flight.* Flight Test Historical Foundation, 1987.

Hansen, James. *Enchanted Rendezvous.* NASA, 1995.

Hendrickson, Walter. *Winging into Space.* Bobbs-Merrill, 1965.

Hunley, J. D. *Toward Mach 2.* NASA, 1999.

Jenkins, Dennis. *Space Shuttle.* Motorbooks, 1993.

Kitmacher, Gary H. *Reference Guide to the International Space Station.* NASA, 2006.

Kohlhase, Charles. *The Voyager Neptune Travel Guide.* NASA, 1989.

Launius, Roger. *NACA to NASA to Now.* NASA, 2022.

Martin Marietta. *Skylab.* Martin Marietta, 1971.

Miller, Jay. *The X-Planes.* Specialty, 1983.

Morrison, David. *Voyages to Saturn.* NASA, 1982.

Morrison. *Voyage to Jupiter.* NASA, 1980.

NASA. *Aboard the Space Shuttle.* NASA, 1980.

NASA. *Artemis Plan.* NASA, 2020.

NASA. *Fifty Years of Aeronautical Research.* NASA, 1967.

NASA. *Industries in Space to Benefit Mankind.* NASA, 1977.

NASA. *Jupiter and Its Moons.* Smithsonian Institution, 1980.

NASA. *Magellan: The Unveiling of Venus.* NASA, 1989.

NASA. *Pioneer Saturn Encounter.* NASA, 1979.

NASA. *Spaceflight: The First 30 Years.* NASA, 1991.

NASA. *The Space Shuttle at Work.* NASA, 1979.

NASA. *This Is NASA.* NASA, 1979.

NASA. *Viking 1: Early Results.* NASA, 1976.

NASA. *Voyager at Neptune.* NASA, 1989.

NASA. *Voyager at Uranus 1986.* NASA, 1985.

NASA. *Voyager: Journey to the Outer Planets.* NASA, 1977.

NASA. *Voyager to Jupiter and Saturn.* NASA, 1977.

Reichardt, Tony. *10: A Decade Aboard America's Space Shuttle.* Final Frontiers, 1994.

Rumerman, Judy, and Stephen Garber. *Chronology of Space Shuttle Flights.* NASA, 2000.

Rycroft, Michael. *The Cambridge Encyclopedia of Space.* Cambridge University Press, 1990.

Shelton, William. *Man's Conquest of Space.* National Geographic Society, 1968.

Siddiqi, Asif. *Beyond Earth.* NASA, 2018.

Smith, Melvyn. *An Illustrated History of the Space Shuttle.* Haynes, 1985.

Sparks, James. *Winged Rocketry.* Dodd, Mead, 1968.

Spilker, Linda. *Passage to a Ringed World.* NASA, 1997.

Young, James. *Meeting the Challenge of Supersonic Flight.* Air Force Flight Center History Office, 1997.

Young, Warren. *To the Moon.* Time-Life Records, 1969.

Books

Bizony, Piers, Andrew Chaikin, and Roger D. Launius. *The NASA Archives: From Project Mercury to Mars Rovers.* Taschen America, 2019.

Bizony. *NASA's Missions to Mars.* Motorbooks, 2022.

Bizony. *NASA Space Shuttle: 40th Anniversary.* Motorbooks, 2021.

Chambers, Mark. *Flight Research at NASA Langley Flight Research Center.* Arcadia, 2007.

Evans, Ben. *NASA's Voyager Missions.* Springer, Praxis, 2022.

Johnson, Katherine. *Reaching for the Moon.* Atheneum Books for Young Readers, 2019.

Jones, Tom. *Space Shuttle Stories: Firsthand Astronaut Accounts from All 135 Missions.* Smithsonian Books, 2023.

Kinney, Jeremy. *Power for Flight.* NASA, 2019.

Miller, Ron. *Curiosity's Mission on Mars.* Twenty-First Century Books, 2014.

Miller. *The History of Rockets.* Franklin Watts, 1999.

Miller. *Robot Explorers.* Twenty-First Century Books, 2007.

Miller. *Rockets.* Twenty-First Century Books, 2007.

Miller. *Satellites.* Twenty-First Century Books, 2007.

Miller. *Space Exploration.* Twenty-First Century Books, 2007.

Miller. *Spaceships.* Smithsonian Books, 2016.

Ross-Nazzal, Jennifer. *Making Space for Women: Stories of Trailblazing Women of NASA's Johnson Space Center.* Texas A&M University Press, 2022.

Websites

International Space Station
https://www.nasa.gov/international-space-station/
Visit the official site for the International Space Station to learn about the station's history and scientific achievements, and to browse the incredible photographs taken by astronauts aboard.

NASA Aeronautics
https://www.nasa.gov/aeronautics/
NASA's aeronautics research is just as crucial as its space program. Visit the official page for its aeronautics information.

NASA History: Johnson Space Center
https://historycollection.jsc.nasa.gov/JSCHistoryPortal/history/nasa_history.htm
The Johnson Space Center website hosts NASA's official history page, which contains links to publications, images, and other information.

The NASA History Series
https://history.nasa.gov/books_home.html
Access more than two hundred books and other NASA publications, most of them for free.

NASA Innovative Advanced Concepts
https://www.nasa.gov/stmd-the-nasa-innovative-advanced-concepts-niac/
This site is devoted to NASA's program to explore daring new ideas by partnering with entrepreneurs and innovators.

NASA's Earth Observing System
https://eospso.nasa.gov/content/nasas-earth-observing-system-project-science-office
The main NASA website for its Earth observation program provides updates and information about the science conducted through satellites orbiting Earth.

NASA Spinoff
https://spinoff.nasa.gov/spinoff/archives
NASA's Spinoff series explores the technologies that have benefited from NASA's contributions and research. All of NASA Spinoff books can be found in this archive in PDF form.

NASA Technology Transfer Program
https://technology.nasa.gov/
Because science is meant to be shared, NASA is dedicated to making its technological innovations available to the public to benefit all of humanity. This website is the home page for its transfer program, where you can access information to utilize many of NASA's technologies for your own projects.

Voyager: Mission Status
https://voyager.jpl.nasa.gov/mission/status/
Where are the Voyager spacecraft now? This site tells you exactly, minute by minute.

Where to Find Mission Raw Images
https://science.nasa.gov/solar-system/moon/where-to-find-mission-raw-images/
This site provides links to sources for raw NASA images from lunar and planetary missions, including the Lunar Reconnaissance Orbiter, Mars's Curiosity rover, and Jupiter's Juno spacecraft.

INDEX

ABOUT THE AUTHOR

Ron Miller is an author and illustrator specializing in science and science fiction. He is the author of more than seventy books, many of them award-winning. He has also designed postage stamps and worked on motion pictures.

For more information about NASA missions, use the QR code:

PHOTO ACKNOWLEDGMENTS

Image credits: © Ron Miller, pp. 6, 46, 82, 95, 125, 137; NACA/NASA, p. 10; Keystone/Getty Images, p. 18; NASA, pp. 20, 27, 32, 44, 56, 65, 73, 86, 88, 106, 113, 115, 128, 133; NASA/Bob Nye, p. 25; NASA/JSC, pp. 37, 38, 60; NASA's Scientific Visualization Studio, p. 39; NASA on The Commons, p. 47; NASA/JSC/Ron Garan, p. 48; NASA/Megan McArthur, p. 61; NASA/GSFC/Solar Dynamics Observatory, p. 70; NASA/JPL-Caltech, p. 74; Enhanced Image by Gerald Eichstadt and Sean Doran (CC BY-NC-SA) based on images provided Courtesy of NASA/JPL-Caltech/SwRI/MSSS, p. 87; NASA/Johns Hopkins University Applied Physics Laboratory/Southwest Research Institute, p. 90; NASA/GSFC/Alex Gerst, p. 97; NASA/Carla Thomas, p. 98; NASA/STScI, p. 104; NASA Image Collection/Alamy, p. 121; NASA/Dave Ryan, p. 123.
Design elements: Arctic-Images/Getty Images; Turac Novruzova/Getty Images; ali gaber/Getty Images.
Cover: NASA.